Version 2.0 - published January 2024

To read this document online, or to check that you are reading the most up-to-date version, visit:
www.themindfulnessinitiative.org/fieldbook-for-mindfulness-innovators

Copyright @ 2024 The Mindfulness Initiative
London, United Kingdom
The Mindfulness Initiative is a Charitable Incorporated Organisation, registered number: 1179834 (England & Wales)

Written by Menka Sanghvi & Jamie Bristow (2019)
Updated by Menka Sanghvi (2024)
Copyedited by Rosie Bell
Design and Illustrations by J-P Stanway

This report should be cited as:
Sanghvi. M, Bristow, J. (2024). Fieldbook for Mindfulness Innovators. The Mindfulness Initiative.
(Originally published 2019)

ISBN 978-1-913353-00-1

 This work is licensed under a Creative Commons Attribution-Non Commercial-NoDerivatives 4.0 International License.

Contributions and support

We thank everyone who has generously contributed their time, expertise and guidance for this resource to be created and made available freely, for the benefit of the wider collective.

Barbara Doeleman-van Veldhoven (Dutch Association for Mindfulness)
Cathy-Mae Karelse (The Mindfulness Initiative)
Chris Cullen (Oxford Mindfulness Centre)
Dan Nixon (Mindfulness Initiative)
David Crook (Starter Culture)
Dean and **Aesha Francis** (Urban Mindfulness Foundation)
Deborah Hardoon (What Works Centre for Wellbeing)
Dusana Dorjee (York University)
Ed Halliwell (Mindfulness teacher)
Jeroen Janss (Inner Green Deal)
Jessica Morey (iBme)
Jonathan Garner (Mind over Tech)
Judson Brewer (Mindsciences.com)
Julieta Galante (Cambridge University)
Katherine Weare (The Mindfulness Initiative)
Luke Doherty (Mindful Peak Performance)
Mari Thorman (HSBC)
Mark Leonard (Mindfulness 4 Change)

Miranda Wolpert (Anna Freud Institute)
Nick Begley (PSYT)
Niraj Shah (Mind Unlocked)
Rebecca Crane (Bangor University)
Richard Burnett (Mindfulness in Schools Project)
Robert Marx (Sussex Mindfulness Centre)
Rohan Gunatillake (Mindfulness Everywhere)
Ruth Baer (Oxford Mindfulness Centre)
Shamash Alidina (Author, Mindfulness for Dummies)
Silvia Brunetti (What Works Centre for Wellbeing)
Singhashri Gazmuri (Mindfulness teacher)
Stephani Unthank-Latter (BAMBA)
Tim Lomas (University of East London)
Vidyamala Burch (Breathworks Foundation)
Vishvapani Blomfield (Mindfulness teacher)

This Fieldbook would not have been possible without the generosity of the Hart Knowe Trust, The Mindful Trust, The Lostand Foundation and Sankalpa, among other valued supporters.

About the Authors

Menka Sanghvi

Menka Sanghvi is a leading voice on creativity and innovation in the mindfulness field. As an interdisciplinary researcher, author and educator, she explores how to design for inner capacities in the digital age. She has led the innovation programme at The Mindfulness Initiative since 2018, creating community resources and developing an awards scheme to improve diversity and inclusion in the sector. Menka is also a podcast host and senior advisor to Mind Over Tech, and a Trustee of the Breathworks Foundation. Menka was previously a global innovation manager at the United Nations and a co-founder of the Impact Hub network. She writes a newsletter about the power of curiosity at *Just Looking*: wearejustlooking.org.

Jamie Bristow

Jamie Bristow is a prominent expert on the application of inner development and contemplative practices in public life. His work includes influential policy reports such as *Reconnection: Meeting the Climate Crisis Inside Out*, and he currently leads on public narrative and policy development for the *Inner Development Goals*, emphasising the inner skills and qualities needed for a sustainable transition. Jamie was Director of The Mindfulness Initiative for eight years, from 2015 to 2023, and played an instrumental role in the *UK's All-Party Parliamentary Group on Mindfulness* during that time. He now retains a part-time position with The Mindfulness Initiative, leading on sustainability policy. Jamie was formerly the Business Development Director at Headspace.

About The Mindfulness Initiative

The Mindfulness Initiative grew out of a programme of mindfulness teaching for politicians in the UK Parliament, and provides the secretariat to the *All-Party Parliamentary Group on Mindfulness*. The Initiative works with legislators around the world who practice mindfulness and helps them to make trainable capacities of heart and mind serious considerations of public policy. It investigates the benefits, limitations, opportunities and challenges in accessing and implementing mindfulness and compassion training and educates leaders, service commissioners and the general public based on these findings. Visit www.themindfulnessinitiative.org to find out more.

Getting in touch

If you have any questions, suggestions or other feedback on this document, please get in touch by emailing info@mindfulnessinitiative.org.uk.

Supporting our work

The Mindfulness Initiative doesn't receive any public funding and in order to retain its neutral and trusted advisory position in the sector, cannot generate revenue from competitive products or services. As such, we are entirely dependent on our supporters for sustaining our charitable work. If you found this document helpful, please consider making a contribution, however small. Visit www.themindfulnessinitiative.org/appeal/donate to make a one-time or recurring donation.

Contributing to this resource

This document is an attempt to codify learnings about mindfulness innovation, so that as a community we do not need to re-invent the wheel each time. To contribute, please get in touch with your feedback, examples and ideas: info@mindfulnessinitiative.org.uk.

Endorsements

❝ The Fieldbook has been an incredibly practical guide for us as we've developed our project, Mindfulness-Based Inclusion Training (MBIT). It speaks to us as innovators creating a unique mindfulness-informed resource that offers guidance and frameworks to nurture human-centred and context-specific training. All whilst still honouring the integrity of mindfulness practice as it continues to evolve and mature and adapt to social contexts.

Aesha Francis and Dean Francis, Founders, Urban Mindfulness Foundation

❝ What a fantastic resource! The Breathworks teaching community has found it really practical, as it is packed with helpful suggestions on how to develop, refine and iterate new ideas.

Vidyamala Burch, Co-founder, Breathworks

❝ Innovative approaches are highly welcomed by eamba to answer the needs of European societies in all their diversity. As eamba we strongly advise mindfulness teachers to explore the Fieldbook for Mindfulness Innovators because it elegantly offers a variety of suggestions to enrich teachers' creative processes and to help bring these processes to fruition.

Katharina Mullen, President of the Board, European Associations for Mindfulness

❝ On our journey of co-creating the Conscious Food Systems Alliance, this Fieldbook was a great support in helping us to plan our initial steps, and to think through the many unknown factors. It continues to be a resource we return to even now, as the Alliance evolves and new ideas emerge.

Dr Thomas Legrand, CoFSA Lead Technical Advisor, UNDP

❝ This is such a great companion for anyone aiming to bring mindfulness to new audiences with care and integrity. It is in itself innovative to have pulled together so many resources, approaches and perspectives in such a usable and accessible way.

Robert Marx, Co-Lead, Sussex Mindfulness Centre

❝ The Fieldbook inspired the creation of the Innovations in Mindfulness Awards. Promoting innovation, whilst respecting what we have inherited, the Fieldbook provided a call to adventure that Mindfulness had been waiting for. The quest to make mindfulness accessible to everyone continues with this revised edition of the Fieldbook.

Vin Harris, Co-Founder, Hart Knowe Trust

Welcome

This Fieldbook was first published in 2019, borne out of a recognition that innovation is both healthy and necessary for mindfulness practices to become more effective and accessible, to target new outcomes, and reach individuals and communities whose needs have not been recognised or met by existing mindfulness-based interventions (MBIs).

Following that publication, the Mindfulness Initiative launched its Innovation Awards in 2022, in collaboration with the Hart Knowe Trust, to promote new approaches in mindfulness that advance the field while ensuring that the standards for MBIs remain as high as possible.

Throughout our work in advancing innovation, we value the strength and efficacy of established evidence-based mindfulness programmes. It is our intention that providing these resources will help mitigate the risk that shallow, ineffective, or even harmful innovations in mindfulness training do a disservice to participants as well as undermine the reputation of the sector. Equally, a sound evidence base can only be the result of sound evidence building, and every new innovation has the potential to enrich this evidence base.

This edition of the Fieldbook includes new research and case studies and also brings to the fore a growing understanding of the wider impact that mindfulness training has, not just at the individualistic level but also societally, helping communities to connect and thrive.

This Fieldbook also holds the criticism that mindfulness training in its dominant form is insufficiently inclusive of and accessible to people of colour as well as those with other minority identities. It calls for innovation that generates a sense of belonging within a diverse society that considers race, identity and culture as vital if we are to face issues of social justice, exclusion, and othering – both historic in nature and current. In the words of Verna Myers, 'If diversity is being invited to the party, inclusion is being asked to dance'. Following this metaphor, it has been suggested that 'belonging is getting to choose the music'.

We hope that reading this Fieldbook encourages you to practise mindfulness at ever-greater depth, turn towards any limitations that you may have in your understanding, collaborate with others, and become a champion for new evidence-building. This is the time to embrace your ambitions and 'choose the music'!

This resource has been made possible through philanthropic support for the Mindfulness Initiative.
If you find it useful and would like to support our future work, please consider making a contribution at
www.themindfulnessinitiative.org/appeal/donate

Richard Edwards|
Director, The Mindfulness Initiative

February, 2024

Content

Introduction

About this book 6

What's in each chapter 6

A mindful approach to innovation 7

Chapter 1
Mindfulness today

1.1 What is mindfulness? 9

1.2 Wider effects 12

1.3 Popular teaching methods 15

1.4 Current evidence 18

Chapter 2
Innovation landscape

2.1 What is innovation? 27

2.2 Different innovation cultures 30

2.3 Opportunities for creativity 32

2.4 Cultivation of teachers 34

2.5 Establishing credibility 38

2.6 Business models 42

Chapter 3
Designing with and for people

3.1 A human-centred approach 47

3.2 Starting with the problem 48

3.3 Co-creating a solution 53

3.4 Awareness of power dynamics 57

3.5 Designing for a Diverse Society 59

Chapter 4
Does it work?

4.1 Why is evidence important? 65

4.2 Early testing and iteration 67

4.3 Explaining how your solution will work 72

4.4 Moving up the evidence hierarchy 74

4.5 Additional resources 80

Chapter 5
The road ahead

5.1 Growing a team 83

5.2 Be a learning organisation 86

5.3 Scaling impact 88

5.4 Deepening practice 90

Introduction

About this book

This book is a result of extensive conversations over the past year with innovators like you who wish to contribute creatively to this growing field, as well as teachers and researchers who care deeply about the integrity and quality of mindfulness innovations.

We recognise that the mindfulness field is developing rapidly with many new research publications, private and public initiatives, organisations and investors frequently arriving in the landscape. We hope to continue our dialogue with innovators and share new information and insights through future iterations of this fieldbook. Check back on the Mindfulness Initiative website for the latest version.

Innovation can be hard and often lonely work. The early stages of innovation can be particularly challenging because of the combination of high uncertainty and low resources. For this reason, much of the material here is focused on the initial development and testing of an idea. Most content applies to innovation in general, but has been curated and adapted to emphasise the elements most relevant for the mindfulness field.

What you will find in this book is not a single 'best practice' model, but many different ideas that you are invited to explore as you navigate the field for yourself. The information shared is necessarily broad and inclusive, to be useful for a wide group of innovators working in a wide range of contexts.

We hope that what follows will serve to enrich your creative work, and that your creativity will in turn enrich the shared knowledge and practices in the field of mindfulness training.

What's in each chapter

Chapter 1
Mindfulness today:
How mindfulness is perceived today and taught, with a focus on secular settings. Includes a definition of a "mindfulness-based approach", details of adaptations, and a summary of the current evidence base for this body of interventions.

Chapter 2
Innovation landscape:
Exploring the main drivers and difficulties of innovation in the field. Includes discussion of exciting opportunities to develop new offerings - as well as challenges such as establishing credibility and developing a business model.

Chapter 3
Designing with and for people:
Key principles and tools of human-centered innovation. Recommended by many disciplines including design, public health policy, and academic research, this approach is equally crucial in the mindfulness training context.

Chapter 4
Making sure it works:
Testing and building evidence. Includes advice on testing assumptions, iterating, validating and establishing a strong foundation of evidence, to build confidence in your approach.

Chapter 5
The road ahead:
Considerations on your onward journey. Introducing some of the challenges and opportunities that lie ahead in the growth of an organisation, platform and team to deliver your innovation into the world.

A mindful approach to innovation

Nine core principles

1. Clarify your intentions: why do you want to innovate?	**2.** Adopt a beginner's mind to explore the problem you wish to solve	**3.** Build on the knowledge and learning that already exist
4. Respect people's understanding of their own needs	**5.** Invite and embrace diverse and challenging voices	**6.** Test and improve rapidly, being prepared to let go of what doesn't work
7. Build your own evidence base so you can be confident in your claims	**8.** Know your limitations: collaborate with others with the skills you need	**9.** Walk the talk: deepen your own personal practice

Chapter 1

Mindfulness today

1.1 What is mindfulness?

Mindfulness is perhaps best considered an inherent human capacity that can be developed through training.

This capacity enables people to attend intentionally **to present-moment experience, inside themselves as well as in their environment, with an attitude of openness, curiosity and care**.

Although we may all be somewhat mindful some of the time, this **state** is hard to sustain and our experience of it may be so rare and fleeting that we do not recognise it. However, we can choose to cultivate and refine this faculty, and the ability to summon and sustain it under various conditions, through **practice**. Mindfulness practices are intentional and regular acts that familiarise the participant with the qualities of mindfulness. These might include formal meditation, mindful pauses or informally remembering to be mindful during the day.

Being mindful does not necessarily involve **meditation**, but for most people this form of mind-training is helpful and required to strengthen the intention and ability to stay present and to cultivate the qualities of mind characteristic of mindful states. Typically, mindfulness meditation guides the participant to focus attention on a chosen object and to observe sensations, thoughts and emotions as events that come and go in awareness. As attention becomes distracted, participants are invited simply to notice that this has happened, and return their focus to their chosen object, with an attitude of kindness.

Many **courses and interventions** guide and support participants to intentionally develop their mindfulness practice and cultivate the trait (and state) of mindfulness. These courses combine formal mindfulness practice with a considerable amount of related psycho-education, and also catalyse the cultivation of capacities such as kindness, gratitude and compassion. Detailed discussion follows in section 1.2.

Further clarification: mind, heart and body

Mindfulness is often described in terms of "training the mind". This can give the false impression that mindfulness is purely about thoughts. Cultivating mindfulness means attuning awareness to all experience including thoughts, but also emotions, body sensations, judgements, sense impressions and so on, as they happen.

> **Mindfulness is a way of being in wise and purposeful relationship with one's experience, both inwardly and outwardly"**
>
> – *Prof. Jon Kabat-Zinn, professor emeritus of medicine and founder of the Center for Mindfulness at the University of Massachusetts Medical School*

Components of mindfulness

We have said that mindfulness is a **capacity for awareness with particular qualities** such as being intentional, present, friendly, open, caring and curious.

More technical definitions of mindfulness categorise these elements as: **intention, attention and attitude**.

Researcher Shauna Shapiro's IAA model illustrates these three elements as interdependent factors occurring not separately but simultaneously.

- *Intention* on purpose, with clarity of personal vision
- *Attention* awareness of one's current experience
- *Attitude* with kindness, openness, curiosity etc.

Similarly, teachers may refer to 'the what and the how' of mindfulness - what we are doing when we are mindful (paying attention) and how we do it (intentionally, with an attitude of, for example, curiosity and care.)

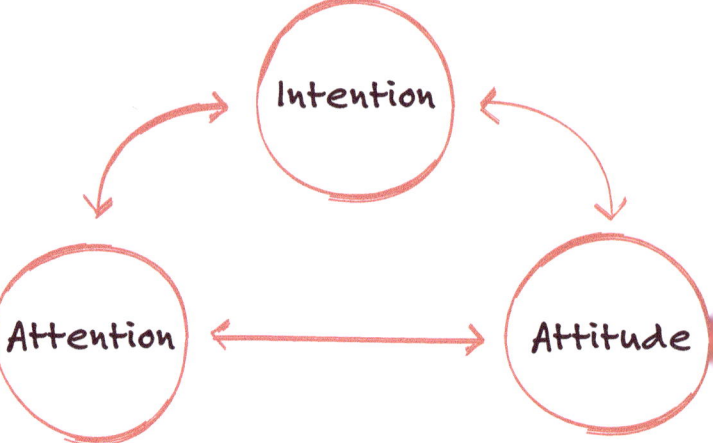

From Shapiro, S., Carlson, L., Astin, J. Freedman, B., (2018) Mechanisms of Mindfulness. Journal of Clinical Psychology

www.semanticscholar.org/author/John-A.-Astin/3657288

Why cultivate mindfulness?

Mindfulness practices have been taught in many contemplative wisdom traditions around the world, most dating back thousands of years. The explicit cultivation of mindfulness is commonly associated with Buddhist traditions, where it forms part of a wider approach to alleviating human suffering. However this history is perhaps better understood as a discovery than an invention. As Brown et.al (2011) remark, "to say that mindfulness is Buddhist is like saying that gravity is Newtonian".

In a dramatic shift over the last 40 years, mindfulness practices have been combined with modern psychological and wellbeing theories, and developed into secular programmes that have been the subject of thousands of scientific trials. Their broad objective in this context remains the alleviation of suffering — whether in a clinical context or in daily life. As these practices have been decoupled from their traditional spiritual context and explained scientifically, they have gained greater reach and popularity than ever before.

Alongside quantified physical and mental health benefits, leading mindfulness programmes emphasise cultivation of the ability to gain perspective, acknowledge and manage emotions, reduce striving, discern wisely in place of snap judgements and automatic reactions, and respond to life situations in calmer, clearer, kinder and more creative ways. Evidence for the benefits of mindfulness is discussed in subsequent chapters.

Although science is helpful to understand and communicate the value in practising mindfulness, academic studies tend to measure individual pathology or performance. We perhaps shouldn't lose sight of mindfulness being an end in itself, helping us to live with greater alertness and presence, enabling us to 'be here' and notice more of our life as it unfolds.

The tendency of research to frame distress within an individual bio-medical paradigm likely also limits the range of options that participants consider when using the greater sensitivity and discernment that come through practice to make positive changes in their lives. Some mindfulness courses are evolving in ways that include wider questions about, for example, society and the environment.

Mindfulness is not relaxation, calm or a quick-fix

Sometimes people are drawn to mindfulness interventions believing that pleasant effects such as relaxation, calm and positive thinking are the goals of practice, and easy to achieve. This misunderstanding of the principles and process of mindfulness can lead to rapid disillusionment, and even feed striving and judgemental tendencies.

> **The essence of mindfulness is not simply to feel "good" as quickly as possible. It is first to cultivate the ability to be fully with our experience as it really is, pleasant or otherwise, with kindness and curiosity, without striving for any particular outcome. As we do so, over time we may indeed find that we more often and more reliably feel calmer, gentler, kinder and more positive. But to experience this or any other benefit takes practice, and this can be a bumpy road. Heightened sensitivity can often mean we experience *increased* suffering at the outset of our journey, which can lead to distress if we misunderstand what it really means to be mindful."**

– *Professor Katherine Weare, Emeritus Professor University of Southampton and Lead for Education at the Mindfulness Initiative*

Key Issue
Many meanings of mindfulness: communicating precisely

The word 'mindfulness' can name several distinct concepts. To avoid confusion and inaccuracy, it is vital when speaking or writing about mindfulness to communicate precisely the meaning we intend, and not to use different meanings interchangeably.

For example, people commonly use the word mindfulness to mean:

- The **state** of being mindful; that is, of attending to present moment experience with curiosity and care

- The general **capacity** or level of ability to be mindful, sometimes called 'trait mindfulness'.

- Mindfulness **practice(s)** such as meditation and informal practice.

- A **training course or intervention** which supports the cultivation of mindful states.

- A **research outcome**. Research scientists have attempted to develop scales which can 'measure' the constituent elements of mindfulness, as a state, capacity or practice using for example self-report questionnaires.

However, be aware that people may also use 'mindfulness' to mean:

- Shorthand for a whole range of techniques and perspectives from **contemplative traditions**.

- Simply being **aware** of something, or being **considerate** – people might say "oops, that wasn't very mindful of me!" when what they mean is that they've been accidentally thoughtless.

- A **social movement** – the cultural phenomenon of Mindfulness (with a capital 'M') in society.

The Mindfulness Initiative / Fieldbook for Mindfulness Innovators

1.2 Wider Effects

Mindfulness is not only of benefit to the individual and their wellbeing. There is a growing awareness of the wider role of mindfulness training in society.

Beyond an individual focus

In many Western societies, individuals are often made to feel singularly responsible for their own wellbeing. This is a feature of the hyper-individualism that underpins so much of modern life. There are concerns that mindfulness practice in these contexts can be framed in a way that limits it to a set of self-help strategies for improving personal mental health and wellbeing, rather than also helping communities and societies to thrive.

For example, in the workplace context, mindfulness is usually promoted as a tool for improving self-regulation - in other words, for remaining calm, focused and productive in the face of difficulties and challenges. This raises a concern about whether mindfulness training may inadvertently encourage people to remain silent about problematic conditions of the workplace and learn to cope on their own rather than raising these issues at an organisational level and finding solutions.

This use of modern mindfulness as a self-help tool to enable better 'functioning' can be traced back to its roots in clinical settings. Mindfulness has been proposed, applied and researched extensively as an effective solution to specific pathologies such as depression, anxiety, stress and so on. The focus in these cases is on individuals using mindfulness practice to take care of themselves rather than addressing societal issues at large.

Recent years have begun to see a shift in this individualistic framing. Several training organisations are now sharing mindfulness practices for the benefit of groups. These more socially focused forms of mindfulness training aim to help people understand their motives and biases towards one another, communicate more effectively, and cultivate a sense of safety and belonging in a team or group, which in turn fosters a culture of wellbeing.

> **Social mindfulness creates a culture where it's recognised that people have difficult feelings and that it is important to express these. It's about having the skills to describe one's own difficult feelings and to listen to others without judgement, or jumping into problem-solving mode."**
>
> – Mark Leonard, curator of socialmindfulness.net and creator of the Mindfulness-Based Organisational Education course.

Societal and planetary wellbeing

Mindfulness training is increasingly recognised as an innate and trainable human capacity foundational to a healthy connection with ourselves but also with others and with nature. These relationships form the bedrock of our behaviour towards the world and underpin our agency to effect meaningful change.

These relationships are intrinsic, for example, to the problem of climate change. While this is an external predicament with physical causes, ecological destruction is rooted in a mindset of separateness that drives social alienation and exploitative human behaviours throughout society, also inhibiting sustainability responses at all levels. The reverse is, thankfully, also true! Mindfulness and compassion practices can restore the kinds of connection to self, others and the world needed to help address the current global sustainability crisis. *The Mindfulness Initiative* publication "Reconnection: Meeting the Climate Crisis Inside Out" gives cause for hope, suggesting the vast inner potential to activate outer change.

Until recently, mainstream mindfulness courses have tended to emphasise the individual - partly because research outcomes are easier to capture at an individual level and partly because public policy organisations and research funders are largely structured with a focus on individual suffering. However, some areas of training demonstrate growing consideration of social context and prosocial behaviour. Concepts such as "social mindfulness" and "ecological mindfulness" represent strands of innovation that are expanding the focus of mindfulness training beyond the individual to wider societal and planetary wellbeing. New research and communication initiatives, such as the *Inner Development Goals*, are highlighting skills and qualities we need to live "purposeful, sustainable and productive lives."

Overview of the Inner Development Goals framework

Being – Relationship to Self	Thinking – Cognitive Skills	Relating – Caring for Other and the World	Collaborating – Social Skills	Acting – Driving Change
- Inner compass	- Critical thinking	- Appreciation	- Communication skills	- Courage
- Integrity and Authenticity	- Complexity awareness	- Connectedness	- Co-creation skills	- Creativity
- Openness and Learning mindset	- Perspective skills	- Humility	- Inclusive mindset and Intercultural competence	- Optimism
- Self-awareness	- Sense-making	- Empathy and Compassion	- Trust	- Perseverance
- Presence	- Long-term orientation and visioning		- Mobilzation skills	

Source: www.innerdevelopmentgoals.org – a non-profit organisation for inner development.

> **Case study**
> **Inner Green Deal**
>
> Inner Green Deal is a non-profit organisation based in Cologne and Brussels with a growing community around the world interested in the human dimension of sustainability. It was founded by Jeroen Janss and Liane Stephan in 2018. They offer capacity-building programmes and curricula for leaders, change-makers and facilitators to accelerate the green transformation. Their partners and clients include the European Union, the Inner Development Goals, and UNDP's Conscious Food Systems Alliance. Their aim is to cultivate the skills and habits needed for collaboration, systems thinking and compassion.
>
> **Developing the leadership capacities needed today**
>
> Jeroen and Liane talk about how today's leaders need to have 'a soft front and a strong back'. The soft front is the humility to be curious, open, and listen deeply to themselves and others. The strong back is the confidence to stand up for what's important, lean into the conversation or the difficulty, and push where needed together with others.
>
> **Research partnership**
>
> From the outset, the Inner Green Deal formed a partnership with the Sustainability Center at Lund University, and has been working closely with Professor Christine Wamsler. One of the outcomes of this partnership has been the development of a new 8-week course: "Mindfulness-Based Sustainable Transformation." The course addresses the sense of overwhelm and anxiety that many experience when thinking about the future, and focuses on strengthening the inner skills necessary for impactful, sustainable action.
>
> To learn more, visit: innergreendeal.com

66 Without inner change, there can be no outer change. Without collective change, no change matters".

– Angel Kyodo Willams

1.3 Popular teaching methods

Mindfulness has been taught in many different ways. Here we explore the arc of mindfulness trainings, from traditional settings to the newer forms of short courses and mobile phone apps.

Tradition-based teaching

For thousands of years the only way of learning explicitly how to cultivate mindfulness involved formal initiation as a student by an experienced spiritual teacher in a contemplative tradition. This method of learning continues to thrive through a wide range of talks, workshops and retreats as well as monastic ordination in many traditions. All of these traditional teaching methods have changed significantly over the years but they tend to remain associated with complex belief systems. Within wisdom traditions, mindfulness practices form part of a much larger whole which encompasses the entirety of life and human experience, lived ethically according to a particular set of beliefs.

Pioneering clinical programmes

Since the late 1970s, mindfulness has been taught in mainstream medical settings. The pioneering secular programme developed at that time by Jon Kabat-Zinn at Massachusetts Medical School is known as Mindfulness-Based Stress Reduction (MBSR), and originally focused on pain reduction. Around twenty years later the Mindfulness-Based Cognitive Therapy (MBCT) programme was developed as a treatment for depression. In the UK, the MBCT course is currently offered to patients through the National Health Service as an evidence-based treatment for recurrent depression.

Both of these clinical interventions generally entail eight weekly classes of up to two and a half hours each. A key reason for this format is its suitability for the clinical healthcare setting. It may not necessarily be the best format in other settings

Over the years these two courses have gathered significant scientific evidence, and have therefore been used as a foundation or template for designing other short courses which cover a wide range of issues, settings and age ranges.

Proliferation of different courses

Most popular modern forms of mindfulness are experienced in a secular setting, with a great many courses available in different contexts and formats, to meet the needs of different populations. Collectively these courses are known as mindfulness-based programmes (MBPs), mindfulness-based applications or approaches (MBAs) and mindfulness-based interventions (MBIs).

Recent years have seen growth in the design of programmes outside clinical healthcare settings. Mindfulness trainings are becoming popular in schools, youth centres, prisons, community centres, and workplaces. Such contexts often require shorter teaching slots to meet particular schedules and cultures. There is usually less emphasis on treating pathologies or illness, and more on promoting strengths such as wellbeing, healthy relationships, creativity, resilience, stress management, focus and practical activity including the performance of tasks.

Mindfulness today

Online platforms and apps

Online teaching through websites, courses and apps is now the norm, and many people learning mindfulness for the first time now do so online, through a mix of live group sessions, community forums, pre-recorded content, and other practices and resources for further support. This format allows students to fit training into their schedules far more easily. It also makes mindfulness more accessible to people living far from training centres or facing mobility challenges. This shift was accelerated by the global pandemic (2020-22) when in-person training was impossible - and since then, many organisations have continued to offer online options.

What about the evidence? While a growing body of evidence suggested the effectiveness of online courses and apps, to date, this medium is not yet considered as effective as the "gold standard" of 8-week in-person courses. However, others point out that the two mediums are not directly comparable. In addition to ease of access, reach and sustainability, online-only training offers distinct benefits compared to in-person courses. One is fidelity and consistency of teaching content (in cases where pre-recorded content is used). Another is the potential of gamification to motivate individuals and establish and maintain their practices. The possibility of tracking every click and interaction, and testing out different teaching methods (A/B testing) with different groups could lead to greater finetuning and effectiveness.

Differentiating programmes

'**Mindfulness-based**' indicates that the core methodology is the practice of mindfulness. Programmes include:

- Mindfulness Based Stress Reduction (MBSR) www.umassmed.edu/cfm

- Mindfulness Based Cognitive Therapy (MBCT) mbct.co.uk/

- Mindfulness Based Pain and Illness Management (MBPM) www.breathworks-mindfulness.org.uk

- Mindfulness Based Living Course (MBLC) www.mindfulnessassociation.net

- Mindfulness Based Childbirth and Parenting (MBCP) www.mindfulbirthing.org

- Mindfulness Based Relapse Prevention (MBRP) www.mindfulrp.com

- Mindfulness-Based Eating Awareness Training (MB-EAT) www.mb-eat.com

- Mindfulness-Based Sustainable Transformation www.mindfulinstitute.org/course-mindfulness-based-sustainable-transformation

In contrast '**mindfulness-informed**' approaches use mindfulness practices within their methodology, and their ethos may also be related to mindfulness, but the core process for supporting people is not a mindfulness practice. Popular mindfulness-informed approaches include:

- Dialectical Behavioural Therapy (DBT)

- Acceptance and Commitment Therapy (ACT)

- Compassion Focused Therapy

- Mindful Self-Compassion self-compassion.org/the-program/

- Somatic Experiencing traumahealing.org/about-us/

- Trauma-Sensitive Mindfulness davidtreleaven.com/

- programmes integrating mindfulness with social and emotional learning/PSHE in schools

- recent examples of developments in the field of Positive Psychology

- Mindfulness-Based Organisational Education www.mindfulnessconnected.com/mboe

What defines a mindfulness-based programme?

In a widely respected paper titled "What defines mindfulness-based programs? The warp and the weft", leading mindfulness innovators and researchers discuss the common features of such programmes. The paper conveys a developing sense of coherence across the diverse mindfulness courses being offered.

The metaphor of 'warp and weft' is used because in weaving, the warp is the fixed thread that runs through the cloth, while the weft is the term for the variable thread in different colours and textures that makes each tapestry unique. For example, the embodiment of qualities of mindfulness in the teacher is considered an essential 'warp' element featuring in all programmes. In contrast, the structure, length and delivery of a programme are adaptable 'weft' elements that make a programme unique and effective for different populations and contexts. These and only these are amenable to innovation.

The features of the warp in the box below make essential reading for innovators: they represent the fundamentals of mindfulness.

Warp	Weft
MBP 1. Is informed by theories and practices that draw from a confluence of contemplative traditions, science, and the major disciplines of medicine, psychology and education	1. The core essential curriculum elements are integrated with adapted curriculum elements, and tailored to specific contexts and populations
2. Is underpinned by a model of human experience which addresses the causes of human distress and the pathways to relieving it	2. Variations in program structure, length and delivery are formatted to fit the population and context
3. Develops a new relationship with experience characterized by present moment focus, decentering and an approach orientation	
4. Supports the development of greater attentional, emotional and behavioral self-regulation, as well as positive qualities such as compassion, wisdom, equanimity.	
5. Engages the participant in a sustained intensive training in mindfulness meditation practice, in an experiential inquiry-based learning process and in exercises to develop insight and understanding	
MBP teacher 1. Has particular competencies which enable the effective delivery of the MBP	1. Has knowledge, experience and professional training related to the specialist populations that the mindfulness-based course will be delivered to
2. Has the capacity to embody the qualities and attitudes of mindfulness within the process of the teaching	2. Has knowledge of relevant underlying theoretical processes which underpin the teaching for particular contexts or populations
3. Has engaged in appropriate training and commits to ongoing good practice	
4. Is part of a participatory learning process with their students, clients or patients	

Full paper: oxfordmindfulness.org/wp-content/uploads/2017/04/16-What-defines-mindfulness-based-programs-the-warp-and-the-weft.pdf

1.4 Current evidence

Many claims are made about the benefits of mindfulness. Not all of these have been proven scientifically. As an innovator in this field it can be tremendously useful to understand what research and evaluation has already been conducted and what evidence there is for certain practices.

Where to go

The most trustworthy and sound evidence in any field is found in studies published in independent academic journals. To publish in a journal takes effort, and papers are assessed and filtered for quality. All respectable journals use blind peer review, which means that an anonymised paper is reviewed by at least two experts in the field. Authors are often asked to make many rounds of corrections, and many papers are rejected altogether.

Be aware, however, that academic journals have their own biases. For example, topics go in and out of fashion with researchers and publishers, and it is often hard to obtain approval for publishing 'nil' results that show no impact. Journals themselves vary greatly in quality, and it is important to rely on those of high reputation.

Where not to go

Online evidence is unfiltered and should therefore be approached with a high degree of scepticism. Given the risk of self-promotion, independent reports by specific mindfulness programmes and initiatives themselves are similarly unreliable.

Overviews

Literature reviews are secondary sources which summarise current knowledge, rather than reporting new or original experimental work. They fall into three broad types:

1. **Narrative reviews** summarise current knowledge including substantive findings, as well as theoretical and methodological contributions to a particular topic. They are sometimes stand-alone pieces, and are appropriate when the field is still developing and there is not much work to report. Selective reviews of a particular topic are usually found at the beginning of a report of a piece of new work, setting the scene for the research that follows.

2. **Systematic reviews** answer a pre-defined research question by collecting and summarizing all empirical evidence that fits pre-defined eligibility criteria, using a transparent and structured methodology to decide what literature to include and exclude. Write-up includes a clear description of the process undertaken. A field must be fairly well developed to yield enough original research papers to make this possible.

3. **Meta-analyses** are systematic reviews which use statistical methods to summarise the results of studies. They bring together the quantitative findings of a range of studies and make a pooled statistical estimate of the overall impact on various outcomes. Likewise they depend upon the existence of enough high-quality studies to make statistical analysis viable.

It is advisable for innovators to keep up with systematic reviews and meta-analyses in the mindfulness field. Below are some recent, good quality examples. Taken together, the evidence they review suggests that standard mindfulness-based interventions (normally eight-week courses) have small but fairly reliable effects on psychological and physical measures of health and wellbeing, in both adults and young people, and that impacts may well be larger for those with greater levels of need. They also suggest that we are beginning to understand the psychological mechanisms that may be at work. All the reviews emphasise the fact there are many methodological weaknesses in the field and that more robust research is needed.

Example meta-analyses in the mindfulness field

Impacts on psychological wellbeing

Khoury, B., Lecomte, T., Fortin, G., Masse, M., Therien. P., Bouchard, V., Chapleau, M., Paquin, K., & Hofmann, S.G. (2013). Mindfulness-based therapy: a comprehensive meta-analysis. Clinical Psychology Review 33, 763–771.

*A total of 209 studies of 12,145 subjects met the inclusion criteria. The findings suggested that mindfulness is an effective treatment for a variety of psychological problems, and is **especially effective for reducing anxiety, depression, and stress**, and as effective as traditional CBT. There were **smaller but still significant effects of in the treatment of physical or medical conditions such as pain and cancer**.*

Bohlmeijer, E., Prenger. R., Taal, E., & Cuijpers. P. (2010). Meta-analysis on the effectiveness of mindfulness-based stress reduction therapy on mental health of adults with a chronic disease. Journal of Psychosomatic Research 69, 614–615.

*A systematic review and meta-analysis examined the effects of MBSR on depression, anxiety, and psychological distress in adults with chronic somatic diseases. The influence of quality of studies on the effects of MBSR was analyzed. Eight published, randomized controlled outcome studies were included. Results showed a **small effect of MBSR on depression and on psychological distress, and a medium effect size for anxiety**, although this result was smaller when studies of lower quality were excluded.*

Kuyken, W., Warren. F., Taylor, R.S., Whalley, B., Crane, C., Bondolfi, G. &, Dalgleish, T. (2016). Efficacy and moderators of mindfulness-based cognitive therapy (MBCT) in prevention of depressive relapse: an individual patient data meta-analysis from randomized trials. Journal of the American Medical Association: Psychiatry. 73(6):565-74.

*Nine randomized trials met the criteria for inclusion, covering 1258 patients with recurrent depression in full or partial remission. Although they found no statistically significant interaction with MBCT treatment overall, there was **some evidence to suggest that a greater severity of depressive symptoms prior to treatment was associated with a larger effect of MBCT compared with other treatments**. The authors concluded that MBCT is an effective treatment for relapse prevention for those with more pronounced residual symptoms of depression.*

Physical indicators of stress and ill health

Heckenberg, R.A., Eddy, P., Kent, S. & Wright. B.J. (2018) Do workplace-based mindfulness meditation programs improve physiological indices of stress? A systematic review and meta-analysis. Journal of Psychosomatic Research (114): 62-71.

*This is the first review to look at the evidence of the effect of MBIs on physiological indices associated with stress and ill-health. The authors concluded that **MBIs were effective in several areas associated with stress reduction and ill health prevention, including reducing cortisol production, improved autonomic balance, improved sympathetic nervous system reactivity and aspects of the immune system**. They deduced that MBIs are a promising avenue for intervention for improving physiological indices of stress and ill health.*

How does mindfulness work?

Gu, J., Strauss, C., Bonda, R., & Cavanagh K (2015). How do mindfulness-based cognitive therapy and mindfulness based stress reduction improve mental health and wellbeing? A systematic review and meta-analysis of mediation studies. Clinical Psychology Review 3: 1–12

> This study aimed to identify potential psychological mechanisms underlying MBCT and MBSR's effects on psychological functioning and wellbeing, and evaluate the strength and consistency of evidence for each mechanism. The review identified strong, **consistent evidence for cognitive and emotional reactivity, moderate and consistent evidence for mindfulness, rumination, and worry**, and preliminary but insufficient evidence for self-compassion and psychological flexibility as mechanisms underlying the effectiveness of MBIs.

Van Der Velden, A.M., Kuyken, W., Wattar, U., Crane, C., Pallesen. K.J., Dahlgaard, J., Fjorback. L.O. & Piet, J. (2015). A systematic review of mechanisms of change in mindfulness-based cognitive therapy in the treatment of recurrent major depressive disorder. Clinical Psychology Review 37: 26–39.

> Twenty three studies were included, 12 of which studies found that **alterations in mindfulness, rumination, worry, compassion, and meta-awareness were associated with MBCT's effect** on treatment outcome for major depressive illness. In addition, preliminary studies indicated that alterations in attention, memory specificity, self-discrepancy, emotional reactivity and momentary positive and negative affect might also play a role in how MBCT exerts its clinical effects.

Impacts on effectiveness in the workplace

Emma Donaldson-Feilder, Rachel Lewis, Joanna Yarker. (2018) What outcomes have mindfulness and meditation interventions for managers and leaders achieved? A systematic review. European Journal of Work and Organizational Psychology 0:0, pages 1-19.

> This review was the first in this field to review research on mindfulness or meditation interventions for managers and leaders. Nineteen studies met the inclusion criteria. **Findings indicated some encouraging signs that mindfulness and meditation interventions may improve aspects of leaders'/managers' well-being and resilience, and leadership capability**, possibly including their "post-conventional" leadership.

Lomas. T., Medina, J.C., Ivtzan, I., Rupprecht, S., & Eiroa-Orosa, F, J. (2018) Mindfulness-based interventions in the workplace: An inclusive systematic review and meta-analysis of their impact upon wellbeing. The Journal of Positive Psychology 74 (4):1-16.

> Eighty one papers met the eligibility criteria, comprising a total of 3,805 participants. **Mindfulness was generally associated with positive outcomes in relation to measures of burnout, distress, anxiety, depression, and stress**. (although results were more equivocal with respect to some outcomes, most notably burnout). The authors concluded that overall, mindfulness appears to improve the well being of healthcare professionals.

Impacts on the young

Dunning. D.L., Griffiths, K., Kuyken, W., Crane, C., Foulkes, L., Parker, J., & Dalgleish, T. (2018). The effects of mindfulness based interventions on cognition and mental health in children and adolescents - a meta analysis of randomized controlled trials. Journal of Child Psychology and Psychiatry. 60(3):244-258

> A systematic literature search of RCTs of MBIs produced 33 studies. Across all RCTs the authors found **significant positive effects of MBIs, relative to controls, for mindfulness, executive functioning, attention, depression, anxiety/stress and negative behaviours**, with small effect sizes. However, when considering only those RCTs with active control groups, significant benefits of an MBI were restricted to the outcomes of mindfulness, depression and anxiety/stress.

Klingbeil, D.A., Renshaw, T.L., Willenbrink, J.B., Copek, R.A., Chan, K., Haddock, and Clifton, J. Mindfulness-based interventions with youth: A comprehensive meta-analysis of group design studies. Journal of School Psychology, 2017. 63: 77-103.

> A meta-analysis of 76 studies in a range of youth related settings concluded that MBIs yield a **small positive average treatment effect across all outcomes, with the largest effect being seen in academic achievement and school functioning, and slightly lower but still positive effects on meta-cognition, attention, cognitive flexibility, emotional/behavioural regulation, distress, depression and anxiety, positive emotions and self-appraisal. It reported larger effect sizes at follow up than immediately after interventions.**

What neuroscience tells us

Deeply important to our understanding of mindfulness training is evidence of 'neuroplasticity': the insight from neuroscience that the structure and function of the brain and nervous system are not fixed in childhood. Human brains are changeable throughout our lives. To some extent, these systems can be re-wired by our behaviours, habits and experiences - including mindfulness meditation - to improve our wellbeing, connection with others, health, happiness and personal effectiveness. As the saying goes, "Neurons that fire together, wire together".

An increasing number of studies, including brain imaging, have explored the impact of mindfulness meditation on brain structures and functions. Cumulative evidence suggests that mindfulness may increase activity (or enhance efficiency) in some brain areas and brain networks and reduce activity in others. The box below shows some of the benefits of these changes in the brain - at least in the short term.

The quantity and scope of neuroscience studies is still quite limited. No neuroscience studies have investigated the long-term effects of mindfulness-based interventions - although studies have taken place with long-term Buddhist meditators. Therefore it is unhelpful to the mindfulness field to exaggerate the weight of neuroscience evidence. Instead, we can support and encourage the growth of this exciting field of research.

Limitations of current neuroscience

Although neuroscientific methods provide useful insights into brain changes associated with mindfulness training, the quantity and scope of existing studies are as yet very limited.

No neuroscience studies have investigated the long-term effects of mindfulness-based interventions, though certain studies have taken place with long-term Buddhist meditators. The long-term effects of mindfulness training on the brain represent an important theme for further research, not least because initial changes in brain structure are likely to significantly recede without sustained meditation practice.

Neuroscience studies are usually conducted with small numbers of participants. To give us more confidence about the impact of mindfulness-based interventions there is a strong need for further studies, repeated studies and those with larger participant samples.

It is unhelpful to the mindfulness field to exaggerate the weight of neuroscientific evidence. While the available findings are certainly interesting, neuroscience of mindfulness is still nascent.

Four brain benefits of mindfulness

Emerging neuroscience research establishes these four benefits of mindfulness practice with reasonable confidence. Treat this as a starting point for further exploring the evidence base and thinking about how your specific innovation might help in similar ways.

1. Attention

The way we pay attention shapes everything about our experience. For many of us, especially in Western culture, our attention is often routinely focused on thoughts. Mindfulness can help us to widen the default sphere of what we pay attention to, and become more aware of other aspects of our experience. This includes, for example, sensations in the body and what is happening in the world around us.

2. Metacognitive awareness

Mindfulness can build our capacity for metacognitive awareness: being aware of how we think. When we are more able to examine thoughts and feelings, we can become less identified with them: in this way, mindfulness can help us "decentre" and loosen the sense of a fixed and immutable self, whose experiences are simply "the way things are". So the capacity for metacognition can ultimately help us embrace a wider perspective, in which we take things less personally and are kinder to ourselves and others, recognising our commonality with other fallible human beings.

3. Emotional regulation

This is the process by which we manage our emotions, becoming aware of them and their impacts on mind and body, relating to them effectively, expressing them appropriately and tracing their roots in the rest of our experience. Through mindfulness practice, we can learn to explore emotions with greater critical awareness. For example, we might interpret some emotional states, such as depressive rumination, as unhelpful passing habits and others, such as righteous indignation, as guides for action.

4. Self-regulation

Self-regulation refers to a cluster of higher-order mental capacities which help us manage our minds, including thoughts, emotions, instincts and actions. Some refer to this as a "master competence" because evidence suggests a strong relationship between levels of self-regulation and positive outcomes for people of all ages - including mental health, wellbeing, relationships and success in life - however we choose to define it.

Reference:

Adapted from The Mindfulness Initiative's document "Implementing Mindfulness in Schools: An Evidence-Based Guide" Weare, K & Bethune, A. (2019)

Avoiding potential harm

So far, we've focused on the benefits. But what about potential harm? Over the years the mindfulness community has been increasingly concerned with the need to take care of, and minimise the potential for any harm. For example, mindfulness training can exacerbate symptoms of traumatic stress. When instructed to pay close, sustained attention to their inner world, those struggling with trauma can experience flashbacks, dysregulation, or dissociation. Research around these concerns is rapidly developing. Overall, the balance of evidence suggests that well-delivered mindfulness programmes can, in fact, help with trauma. Nevertheless, more and more training programmes are wisely adapting to become more "trauma-informed", to reduce the risk of harm as much as possible. As an innovator, it is worth taking the time to consider carefully what measures you might take to build safety, trustworthiness and empowerment in your approach.

Explore Further
Managing Risks

David Treleaven's website davidtreleaven.com and book Treleaven, D. A. (2018). Trauma-sensitive mindfulness: Practices for safe and transformative healing.

An article from the Oxford Mindfulness Centre with a list of research on the subject: oxfordmindfulness.org/news/is-mindfulness-safe

Meditation safety toolbox from Brown University with documents, protocols and best practice guidelines developed by learning mindfulness researchers.
brown.edu/research/labs/britton/resources/meditation-safety-toolbox

Take care when claiming equivalence

The term "mindfulness" is now used to describe all kinds of practices, many of which would more accurately be described simply as 'attention training' or 'relaxation exercises'. Most of the evidence-based benefits of mindfulness described in this chapter refer to high-quality training programmes that cultivate mindfulness over longer periods of time, such as the 8-week MBSR, MBCT or Breathworks courses. Other studies have been based on intensive five or ten-day meditation retreats. These are the specific versions of mindfulness training that have been carefully evaluated. It is questionable whether the exact same benefits can be gained from other programmes, online resources or apps. That's not to say that they won't be helpful, but it does mean that it is misleading to cite benefits that are extrapolated from the scientific evidence base to make claims.

Case study
Inappropriate comparisons

In 2006 researcher Sarah Bowen and colleagues published a study that showed that teaching meditation to prison inmates through a ten-day intensive retreat reduced drug and alcohol usage when these prisoners were released from jail, as compared to their peers who hadn't meditated. This led to the development of a Mindfulness-Based Relapse Prevention programme. When this same research was quoted by a mindfulness company claiming that their smartphone app could help people overcome addiction issues, the researchers of the study responded saying that this might be an "overinterpretation or misrepresentation" because "we don't have the data on that."

Source: www.mindful.org/can-your-smartphone-make-you-mindful/

Tool box
Keeping up with scientific evidence

To explore the latest research yourself, search online indexes for 'mindfulness', 'systematic reviews', 'meta-analysis', and other terms in your specific interest area - ideally over the past 2-3 years. When researching the background to particular innovations, you may need to search for research papers on a particular topic using keywords.

Two good quality and much-used indexes that bring together published papers are PyscINFO run by the American Psychological Association, and PubMed by the US National Library of Medicine. Both of these are to be preferred to the less reliable Google Scholar: you may want to look at all three.

The journal 'Mindfulness' published by Springer is generally thought to be the most reputable in the field and well worth keeping up with.

Some research papers will be freely accessible, but some are behind paywalls or require membership to certain sites. Universities generally pay high fees so that their staff and students can access journal databases. However, academic papers can be viewed via the online 'research rental service' DeepDyve.com for a monthly subscription.

Papers may also be available on MindRxiv mindrxiv.org/, an open archive for research on mind and contemplative practices. Many researchers working in the area upload their published articles or 'preprints' (a version that hasn't been edited and copyrighted by academic journals) to this database, available for free.

'AMRA', the American Mindfulness Research Association, provides monthly newsletters summarising the latest research as part of a paid subscription via goamra.org. This may be the most time-efficient way of keeping track of developments. Mindful Magazine and Mindful Digital also regularly publish articles on the most exciting new science. www.mindful.org

When planning innovation or evaluation in a particular field it is helpful to involve experts within universities or other research establishments who are familiar with the existing literature.

Other helpful resources include: National Center for Complementary and Integrative Health (NCCIH) Research Results / National Center for Complementary and Integrative Health (NCCIH) Clearinghouse / ISCMR Research Resources / Greater Good Science Center / Center for Healthy Minds / Collaborative for Academic, Social and Emotional Learning (CASEL).

Why are mindfulness courses effective?

One of the challenges of research in this area is the difficulty of pinning down exactly which element of an intervention is to be credited for any benefits. For example, imagine a mindfulness course for a group of teenagers suffering from low self-compassion appears to produce successful results. This might be due to the psychological education that was received, the social benefits of being part of a peer-group, the actual practices of mindfulness, a combination of these, or something else entirely!

We could describe the specific aspects of an intervention responsible for its positive impact as 'active ingredients' (a term originally used in medical trials). There are different views on what these ingredients are, and we are still learning. Identifying them is important because the more effort is devoted to the elements that are actually responsible for beneficial outcomes, the more effective your programme will be.

Mindfulness teachers with considerable on-the-ground experience assert that the deeper fruits of practice are only available through courses of at least six weekly sessions of a few hours each, with practices lasting at least 20 minutes. This is due to the necessity for participants to start encountering and working through their own resistance and reactivity in relation to practice. Published evidence is emerging to support this view - see for example Parsons, C. E. et al (2017) 'Home Practice in Mindfulness-Based Cognitive Therapy and Mindfulness-Based Stress Reduction: A systematic review and meta-analysis of participants' mindfulness practice and its association with outcomes'. Behavioural Research Therapy 95:29-41.

Key Issue
Active ingredients

Active ingredients are the specific aspects of an intervention that are responsible for its positive impact.

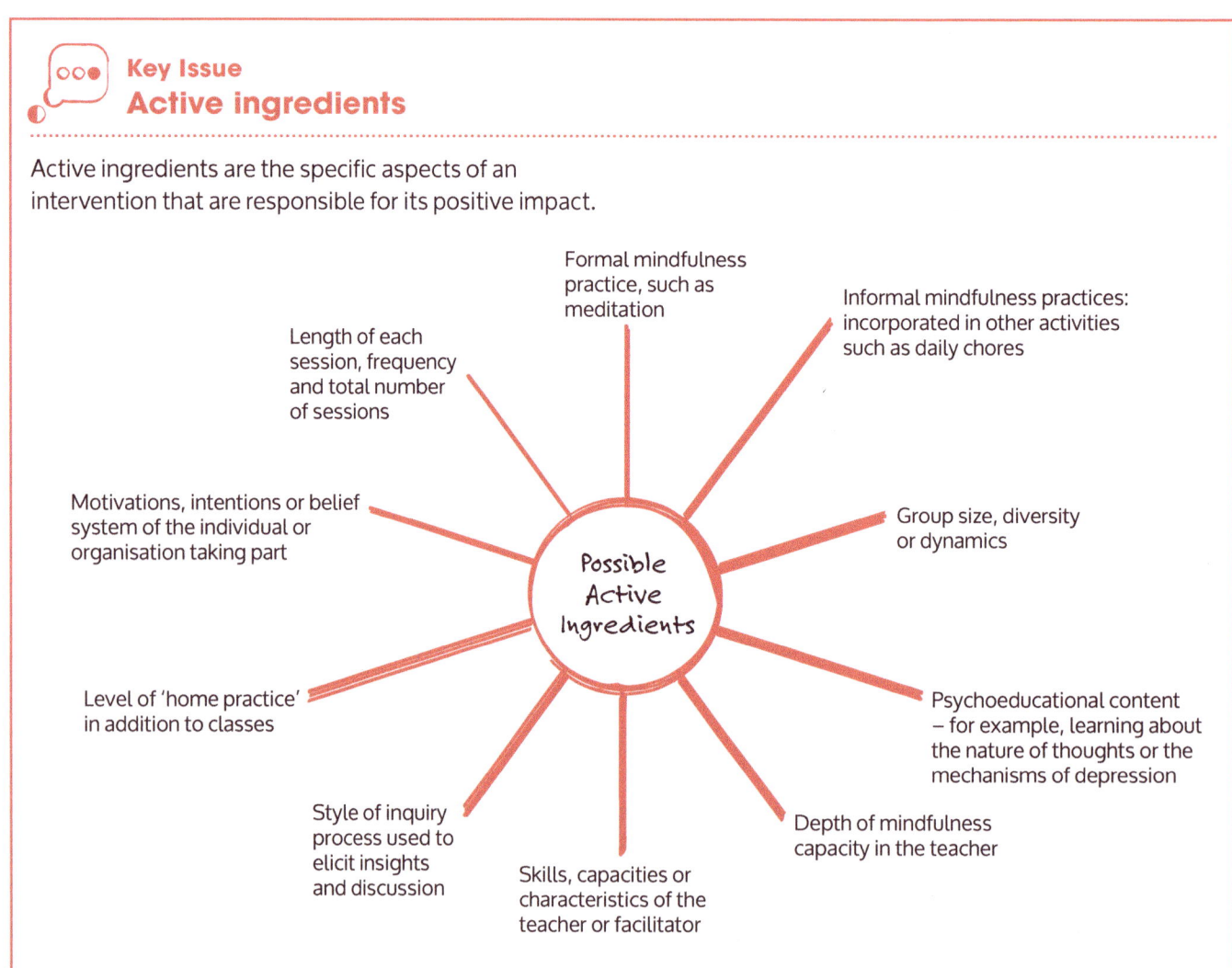

> **Evidence is not able to keep up so we don't know if a lot of the newer creative approaches are working, or not."**

– Professor Willem Kuyken, Oxford Mindfulness Centre

Chapter 2

Innovation landscape

2.1 What is innovation?

Innovation as a process for overcoming challenges

Innovation is a creative approach to problem-solving: a process that starts with people and their needs, and ends with new solutions that meet those needs. The result can be a new kind of product or service, process, position or even a whole new paradigm.

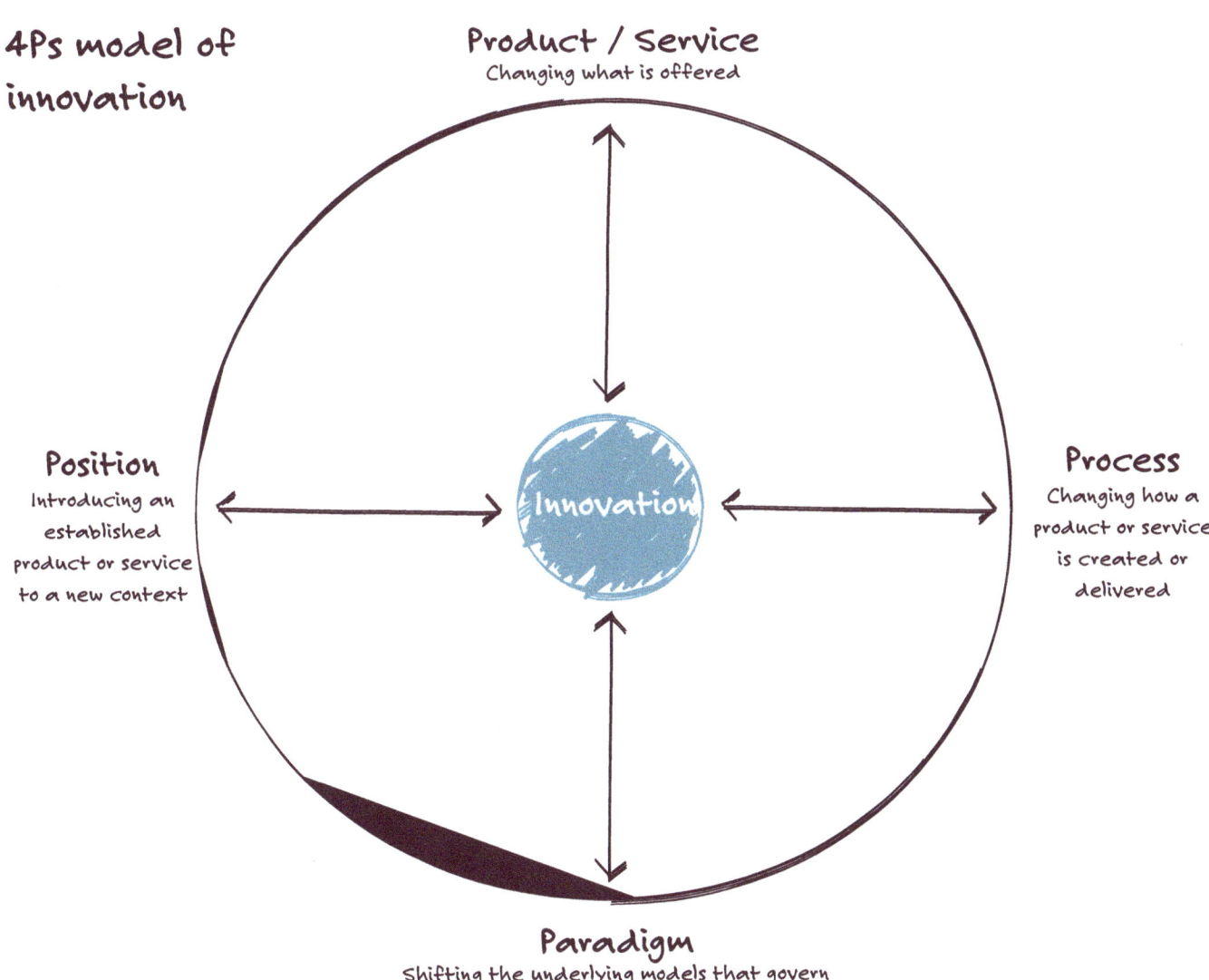

Source: Francis and Bessant
www.researchgate.net/publication/223832747_Targeting_Innovation_and_Implications_for_Capability_Development

Innovation landscape

One of the UK's leading innovation organisations, Nesta, has created a useful map that helps innovators to look ahead and plan their journey. The adapted extract below illustrates the stages of the process. You can use this to check where you are in your process, and whether you have included all of the necessary considerations in your plan.

Source: Adapted from Nesta (2013) Innovation Flowchart. diytoolkit.org/tools/innovation-flowchart-2/

Stage	Skills required	Examples of activity	Kinds of evidence generated	Goal
Exploring opportunities & challenges	Research (formal and informal)	Collecting input from others, including the people who experience the problem you are trying to solve	Insights derived from formal research and informal knowledge-gathering	A well understood and clearly defined problem or opportunity
Generating ideas	Creativity, facilitation	Ideas generation, including working together with the people who experience the problem	Theory of change: a clear account of likely causation supported by evidence	A set of ideas to develop and test
Developing & testing	Design, implementation, research, partnerships	Using prototypes to quickly test out initial ideas, and then engaging in deeper research to find out if they work	Practical trials and experiments involving potential users (beneficiaries) of the innovation	Demonstration that the idea works, or evidence to support a reworking of the idea
Making the case	Business development and evaluation	Developing a business model	Stronger case with cost and benefit analysis	Clarity about what warrants implementation and funding
Delivering & implementing	Strong leadership, management and implementation skills	Implementing the programme with a target group	Robust and detailed analysis of outcome, through formal evaluation and evidence gathering. Use of a control group to isolate impact	A credible, implementable and sustainable innovation
Growing, scaling and spreading	Strong leadership and management skills	Developing a business plan and raising finance	Evidence derived from evaluations in multiple sites, and independently run randomised control trials	Innovation or impact at scale
Changing systems	Identification and training of new leaders and teams	Building partnerships	New definitions and measures for efficiency and impact created	A transformation in the way we do things

Innovation as a set of behaviours

As well as a process, innovation may be approached as a group of behaviours, including keen observation, open-mindedness, risk-taking and ready adaptation.

When trying to understand a problem, successful innovators typically adopt a 'beginner's mind', suspending judgement and looking at a situation with fresh eyes. One of the most common errors made in innovation is jumping to solutions too quickly, without taking the time to examine the problem thoroughly enough.

While developing solutions, innovators need patience, humility, and strong listening skills in order to understand feedback and improve the offering.

Innovation involves a great deal of uncertainty and risk. If there is no chance of failure, then it's likely that nothing new is really being attempted. The successful innovator must have the courage both to create and to let go of anything that doesn't work.

> **The process of innovation should feel uncomfortable. It goes against our habit and instinct which is to find a solution, which is a somewhat fear-based response. The whole point is to give yourself space to get lost and wander out. Just to be present with what's here now, without any preconceived outcomes."**
>
> – Jonathan Garner, founder of Mind over Tech

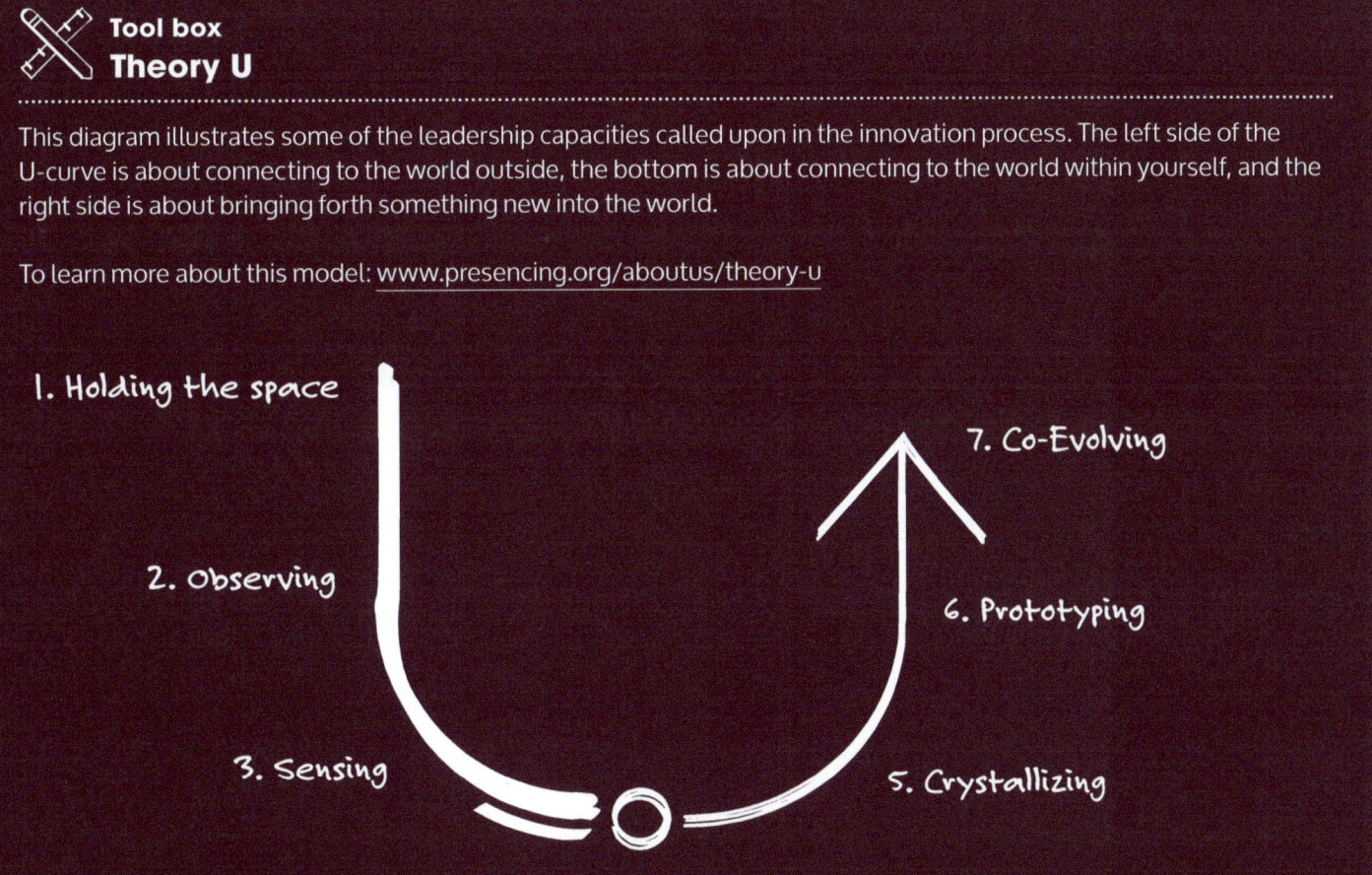

Tool box: Theory U

This diagram illustrates some of the leadership capacities called upon in the innovation process. The left side of the U-curve is about connecting to the world outside, the bottom is about connecting to the world within yourself, and the right side is about bringing forth something new into the world.

To learn more about this model: www.presencing.org/aboutus/theory-u

1. Holding the space
2. Observing
3. Sensing
4. Presencing
5. Crystallizing
6. Prototyping
7. Co-Evolving

Source: 'Theory U: Leading from the Future as It Emerges' by Otto Scharmer.

2.2 Different innovation cultures

Within the mindfulness field there are many different cultures around innovation. Broadly, these cultures can be grouped into three areas: traditional, academic and entrepreneurial. In general, while the depth and expertise is held by communities in tradition-led and academic institutes, these groups tend to be quite conservative and slow in developing new approaches. There is also a tension between the entrepreneurial spirit of wanting to do things quickly and efficiently, and the academic mindset which puts more value on rigour and depth.

While each culture has its strengths, their differences lead to siloed approaches at a cost to the overall quality of innovation in the space. This is why, as an innovator, it can be incredibly useful to understand and try and build bridges between them.

Traditional

Over the centuries there have been significant innovations in the ways that religious and spiritual groups have encouraged the cultivation of mindfulness. Great efforts have been made to translate key concepts in a way that more people can understand and relate to. In general, however, these changes occur slowly and gradually over the lifetime of highly experienced teachers.

Academic

Pioneering secular programmes have emerged from rigorous academic research and analysis in therapeutic settings. For example, MBCT came from mapping psychological theories about recurrent depression with mindfulness practices. Over the years many other innovations have taken place, but in loyalty to the evidence new programmes tend to be quite closely aligned with the original MBCT and MBSR approaches. Emphasis is more on "skillful adaptations" than on exploring creative departures from the status-quo.

Reliable research on new approaches takes several years to complete, which limits the pace of innovation. Research findings have been used to inform and iterate new approaches, but it can be a relatively slow and expensive process. For example, the MBCT course was carefully developed over a period of 30 years. Currently research on mindfulness in schools is generating some reliable conclusions based on studying the work of 30 different MBIs over the last 10 years.

Entrepreneurial

The consumer space has seen the introduction of hundreds of mindfulness books, courses and apps, many achieving commercial success and scale. Offerings of this kind are often developed and launched within a matter of months or a few years. Millions of people have discovered mindfulness because of these accessible and user-friendly products and services.

Popularity is not necessarily an indicator of effectiveness. The terms "pop mindfulness" and "McMindfulness" point to concerns around mindfulness products designed to be cost-effective and scalable for a large audience, with insufficient consideration of quality and impact.

Mindfulness apps have been a particular source of debate. Some critics note that when apps treat mindfulness guidance as "content", users may just listen passively, rather than actively participating. Others worry that encouraging users to rely on an app prevents them from learning to practice independently.

Incentives to invest in scientific evidence are limited in non-regulated consumer markets. Where empirical research on outcomes is conducted - for example on mental health and wellbeing - it is often carried out after the intervention has already proven commercially successful, with a large number of customers already using the service.

> **If things continue as they are .... then we will see the mindfulness world break apart completely into large-scale mindfulness products which lack deep understanding of the practice, ivory-tower academics doing good work but not being heard because it's not being integrated into products for the marketplace, and spiritual communities becoming even more niche than they are now as the connections between pop mindfulness and spiritual practice become more and more diluted. More importantly, if things continue as they are, everyday people miss out. The only mindfulness they will encounter will be the best marketed mindfulness, not necessarily the best quality mindfulness."**

– *Rohan Gunatillake, creator of mindfulness app, Buddhify.*
Source: buddhify.com/the-missing-middle-of-modern-meditation-and-how-to-fill-it/

Culture	Led by	Main influences	Time scale for innovation	Use of technology	Primary relationship
Traditional	Contemplative or spiritual teachers	Teachings from those considered more experienced on the path	Slow and gradual, only changing as little as necessary to meet new needs. Major changes have taken hundreds of years	Cautious and concerned about the impact of tech. Focus more on workshops and retreat settings.	Teacher and student
Academic	Theorists, researchers and therapists	Compelling scientific theories and evidence	Depending on the length of experiments, it can take several years to establish robust evidence	Mixed but interventions and programmes tend to be mostly in person and tech-free	Facilitator or teacher and participant
Entrepreneurial	Social entrepreneurs, investors, technologists	Current culture and needs and what will succeed in the market	Months or years from initial conception to launch of product or service	Embracing all forms of technology as a means of delivering impact	Content provider with user or consumer

2.3 Opportunities for creativity

Innovation is the spirit of wanting to make things better, and to make better things. Its most common driver is direct observation that current approaches to meeting a need are not 'good enough', or the persistent sense that there may be a more powerful possibility. As with every emerging field, there are many ways in which the modern field of mindfulness would benefit from innovation.

We asked several leading thinkers in the space about what some of these potential areas of possibility might be, and the following is a summary of their responses. Each door you might open leads to an exciting and complex set of possibilities.

Reasons to innovate

1. **Inclusion of different groups of people**

    Cultural, economic and ethnic diversity
    Mindfulness practice seems to be growing faster in certain demographics, particularly affluent, middle-class white people. Reaching a greater diversity of people from different socio-economic, ethnic and cultural backgrounds is likely to require creativity, participatory engagement, and the development of new approaches.

    Professional context
    There may be an opportunity for mindfulness courses to better address the specific challenges faced in different professions. The variation in culture and performance demands across sectors means that interventions may need different structures, language and outcome priorities.

    Different styles of learning
    New approaches for sharing mindfulness could be tailored to individual differences, such as personality, literacy and learning preferences. This would require going back to the drawing board with some of the core ways in which mindfulness is currently being taught.

    Vulnerable groups
    Many teachers of mindfulness are keen to see the practices benefiting the most vulnerable groups in society. For example, using mindfulness to support trauma-sensitive interventions for high-risk groups including abused children, refugees and prisoners. This kind of work would require very skillful teaching to avoid causing any additional harm.

2. **Addressing a wider range of social issues**

    Helping entire communities, not just individuals
    Mindfulness could be powerful not just in addressing individual distress but also on a community or societal level. Currently there are hopes that this effect will emerge naturally through "bottom up" engagement, but certain innovators are more actively trying to develop methods of teaching which directly target groups, such as families, organisations, neighbourhoods or towns, addressing their context.

    Tackling underlying causes of suffering in society
    Mental health strategies attract criticism from those who believe that they place too much emphasis on the individual and not enough on wider societal drivers of poor mental health, such as racism, inequality, educational approaches, lack of green spaces, working culture, etc. Mindfulness can offer a dual focus, facilitating shifts in people's internal and external circumstances.

    Supporting social and political influencers
    Some innovators are looking at how to support policy makers, activists, and social entrepreneurs to use mindfulness as an inner and outer growth strategy. Emergent examples include the Oxford Mindfulness Centre's work with politicians.

    Values, ethics and prosocial behaviour
    Many of the positive changes that we desire as a society, for example tackling climate change

and environmental degradation, or addressing homelessness and poverty, require a shift in individual and group values, ethics and behaviour. Research evidence suggests that this is an area in which mindfulness may be supportive, both directly and indirectly encouraging these shifts.

Creating mindful environments
Through mindful experience design, scaled to apply to mindful architecture, mindful environments, mindful schools and mindful cities, might we create environments that nudge us to live more mindfully?

3. Expanding and deepening the possibilities of practice

Going deeper
Although the 8-week courses are considered "gold standard", there is not enough time to maximise the potential of the practices. The richer fruits of practice over a lifetime have been evidenced in subjective reports, and some neuroscientific studies on long-term meditators. Taught over longer periods of time, advanced practices appear not just to help people to cope, but also to address underlying causes of distress and enable people to lead fuller, more deeply realised and ethical lives.

Secularisation of further traditional practices
Mindfulness practices exist in many contemplative traditions such as Buddhism, Christianity, Islam, Judaism, Jainism, Sufism etc. Through deeper exploration of these traditions it may be possible to teach a wider range of practices in secular settings.

Informal practices
There is huge potential for the development of more informal mindfulness techniques that can be practised throughout the day, particularly given the current rate of change in culture and lifestyle.

Community aspect
Strengthening the social dimension of mindfulness programmes could help people to connect and build communities of support for their mindfulness practice. For example, there are currently very few models or platforms that encourage the community aspect to continue after an 8-week course has finished.

Interdisciplinary insights
Incorporating insights from parallel disciplines and sectors such as positive psychology, neuroscience and behavioural economics into mindfulness teachings is an ongoing and fruitful process, and work is emerging on these important connections.

4. Embracing new technology

Positive education around tech use
As people are increasingly overwhelmed by information, device addictions and stress from social media, there is a growing need for mindful practices to embrace technology, helping us to integrate its use in our lives in healthy ways.

Going digitally native
The cultivation of mindfulness could go beyond the simple guided content consumption that is prevalent in existing apps and online courses. This might involve using the technology itself to train the mind in attention and awareness.

Mindful design
The business models behind many new ventures - especially smartphone apps - are based on attention capture and retention, provoking concern about individual agency and the fragmentation of minds. In response, a social movement is evolving towards being more respectful of human attention. There is a strong case for alternative business models that do not exploit our vulnerabilities. Mindfulness might also be considered in the design of products, services and environments.

Responding to artificial intelligence
With technological advances such as artificial intelligence and many analytic jobs being taken over by robots, the importance of mindfulness capacities will increase as a source of advantageous differentiation.

Neurofeedback
Drawing parallels with the use of biofeedback in the physical fitness world, innovators are now looking into how neurofeedback can be used in meaningful ways. Achieving this in an accessible, affordable way will be a further challenge.

> **We can bake the bread using an old recipe but using the ingredients of 'now'.**
>
> – Ed Halliwell, *mindfulness teacher*

2.4 Cultivation of teachers

Scalability

Teachers and facilitators are a core requirement and a core cost for the delivery of most mindfulness programmes, products and services. The extent to which any offering scales therefore depends heavily on the way teaching is structured. The following case study illustrates what can happen when teaching capacity receives insufficient consideration and investment.

Risks of poor teaching

Mindfulness practice is sometimes compared to physical exercise: there are many great benefits but the exercises must be done carefully to avoid the risk of harm. Mindfulness is a subtle practice and it is generally accepted that it can only be taught well by people with considerable personal understanding and experience. As a result, there is justified concern about teaching quality and integrity.

Safety concerns are especially important when teaching more intense practices that, for example, encourage participants to bring attention to unpleasant experiences. Often the changed perception of pain can make it feel worse temporarily as students pay attention to it and learn to manage it. The responsibilities are even greater when working with vulnerable people who are already suffering physically or mentally. Teachers must be trauma-aware and able to support participants in ways that avoid harm.

Also significant is the risk that practices may be diluted or misapplied to the extent that they are no longer effective. For some participants this may be the only or last attempt they make to benefit from mindfulness practice, representing an enormous opportunity lost if it doesn't work.

Explore further
Why, When and How to Adapt?

More and more mindfulness teacher training now addresses the topic of how teachers can adapt content to suit their audience. This area of training aims to equip teachers to adapt skillfully - and to appreciate the compromises that may be implicit in doing so. One useful resource that tackles this question is: "Mindfulness-Based Programmes: Why, When and How to Adapt?" Loucks EB, Crane RS, Sanghvi MA, et al. Mindfulness-based programs: Why, when, and how to adapt? *Glob Adv Health Med.* 2022;11:21649561211068805.

> **It is important to have disclaimers around mental health, and where possible to clearly say that this app or event may not be suitable for you if you have certain serious conditions. We point people towards the NICE guidelines for mental health, and where appropriate encourage people to seek specialist help, which we currently do not offer."**

– Niraj Shah, founder of Mind: Unlocked

Different models for cultivating teachers

Several approaches to building teaching capacity have emerged within the sector, each with its own strengths and weaknesses. From a sector perspective it is thought that we need a range of such approaches to enable both the depth and breadth of teaching. Considering which approach would best suit your innovation from the earliest stages of idea development may be helpful.

1. **Teacher Training Model**
   There are internationally well-established models for training people to teach empirically validated programs. The teaching process allows room for variation, as it is designed to be highly responsive to what is arising in the moment, and each teacher needs to find their own voice and personhood to enable an authentic teaching process. These teaching and training models encourage high standards in quality and consistency, and are known to be effective for participants. There are however contexts, populations and particular aims for MBP delivery for which these models are not likely to be the best fit. So it is important to explore other methodologies for training and teaching, in parallel.

   Examples: MBCT / MBSR / Breathworks/ Mindfulness in schools project (.b, .Paws etc.) / Mindful Self-Compassion / most taught courses

2. **Peer mentoring schemes**
   This approach focuses on educating and empowering people to share informally what they have learnt with their peer group. As well as costing less, the distinct advantage of this approach is that it benefits from the strength of existing relationships: people learn best from people they already know or can relate easily to.

   Examples: Sharing Mindfulness (Wales) / Thought on a Thread (South Africa) and HSBC Mindfulness at Work Champions Model (Global) / Buddhify Transmit.

3. **Open creative approach**
   This approach trains teachers not just to deliver one particular fixed curriculum, but how to creatively and skillfully adapt the materials and delivery style to suit the population and context in hand. This is sometimes known as an "embedded approach" and has the advantage of rapid diversification, but with the risk of ineffective adaptations.

   Examples: Sussex Mindfulness Centre's training programme in adapted mindfulness-based interventions (MBIs) / Mindfulness Training Institute

Innovation landscape

4. **Train the trainer**
   Creating more teacher trainers facilitates faster growth in new teacher numbers, because each graduate can immediately go on to train others. The concern with this approach is that being a 'trainer' (teaching others how to teach) requires additional skills to simply being a good teacher, and if these are overlooked then over time the quality of teaching and benefit to participants would become diluted.

   Examples: Mindfulness Training for First Responders (USA)/ Breathworks

5. **Plug and play model**
   The challenge of teaching capacity is sidestepped to an extent by online services and apps, where content is carefully developed and recorded in advance, and can be played on demand. While this ensures consistency and high quality in one regard, the absence of a teacher's physical presence, modelling a way of being, answering questions and adapting content in response to a specific group is a huge deficit.

   Examples: Mindfulness Without Borders / Headspace / Calm / Be Mindful Online / most mindfulness apps

> **Some training offers prescribed teaching content, while others allow more teacher flexibility. Whatever one thinks about particular training methods, the general principle I would apply is that the level of training should match the level of delivery, and that we should be aware of what is lost and gained in each case. Honestly recognising these trade-offs can lead to further innovation."**
>
> – Vishvapani Blomfield, Mindfulness teacher and founder of Sharing Mindfulness (Wales)

Case study
Building on existing relationships: BAM!

The Peak Mindfulness programme BAM! (Boxing and Mindfulness) emerged from a realisation that hard-to-reach young people are unlikely to engage in a mindfulness session, even if offered for free. Founder Luke Doherty came up with the idea of combining mindfulness with non-contact boxing, which made the training more relevant and accessible to people who wouldn't normally be interested in mindfulness.

To deliver this mindfulness training, Luke worked collaboratively from the outset, with boxing clubs such as the East London Boxing Academy, whose coaches already had a close relationship with hard-to-reach young people.

As his organisation grew, Luke and the team started to train and establish their own BAM! qualified instructors who could travel to different places and teach young people. However, they soon found it was more effective to train existing boxing coaches, youth workers, and mental health practitioners in delivering their approach, since these people already had the relationship, rapport and trust with the intended audience. So Luke and his team pivoted their model to providing teacher training to existing organisations.

Peak Mindfulness is currently working with the charity Mind to train their staff to use boxing, as well as a wider range of body movements, as mental health support tools. Their training is being developed with coproduction from service users and clinical input from Mind. In its current format, 2.5-days of training are spread over six weeks, with an additional Continued Professional Development aspect. The aim is for Mind staff to build their personal knowledge and confidence to deliver the BAM! approach.

To learn more, visit: mindfulpeakperformance.com/community

Case study
HSBC's Employee-Driven mindfulness ecosystem

Within HSBC, an employee initiative known as "Mindfulness@hsbc" was created by Mari Thorman in 2011. It began as a grassroots project to provide access to mindfulness resources for all staff, regardless of work area, grade, background, etc. The offerings ranged from short taster sessions and events, guided sessions and apps to access to further education through longer courses provided by an external mindfulness trainer.

Champion-led model

To sustainably scale the access to these resources across HSBC, a new model was piloted in 2017, and the community has been growing since. It is based on "champions" who are volunteer employees passionate about sharing mindfulness practice with others. After completing a 6-module Mindfulness Foundations course, these champions can pursue 3 further training levels:

Level 1 - Facilitator - trained to guide mindfulness sessions and deliver talks and introductions to colleagues across the business

Level 2 - Leader - trained to deliver courses to colleagues and mentor new Champions.

Level 3 - Principal - qualified to deliver all levels of Champion training and serve as a mentor and consultant for innovations, ethics and quality guidance.

Having these different levels protects the quality and depth of how mindfulness is shared and taught while allowing for cost-effective growth across the organisation. Courses, awareness and practice sessions have been delivered to over 40,000 employees since the network's inception. This impressive impact has led to the programme becoming a permanent business offering, with a support team in place.

Further adaptations

HSBC has many different kinds of business units, each with its own culture and pressures. The mindfulness course, therefore, needs to be adapted from time to time, both in terms of content and delivery style. For example, in some cases, it makes more sense for teams to learn mindfulness together, whereas in others, it is more of an individual leadership exercise. A small central function provides coordination, support and consultancy to encourage appropriate adaptations without compromising the integrity of the original curriculum.

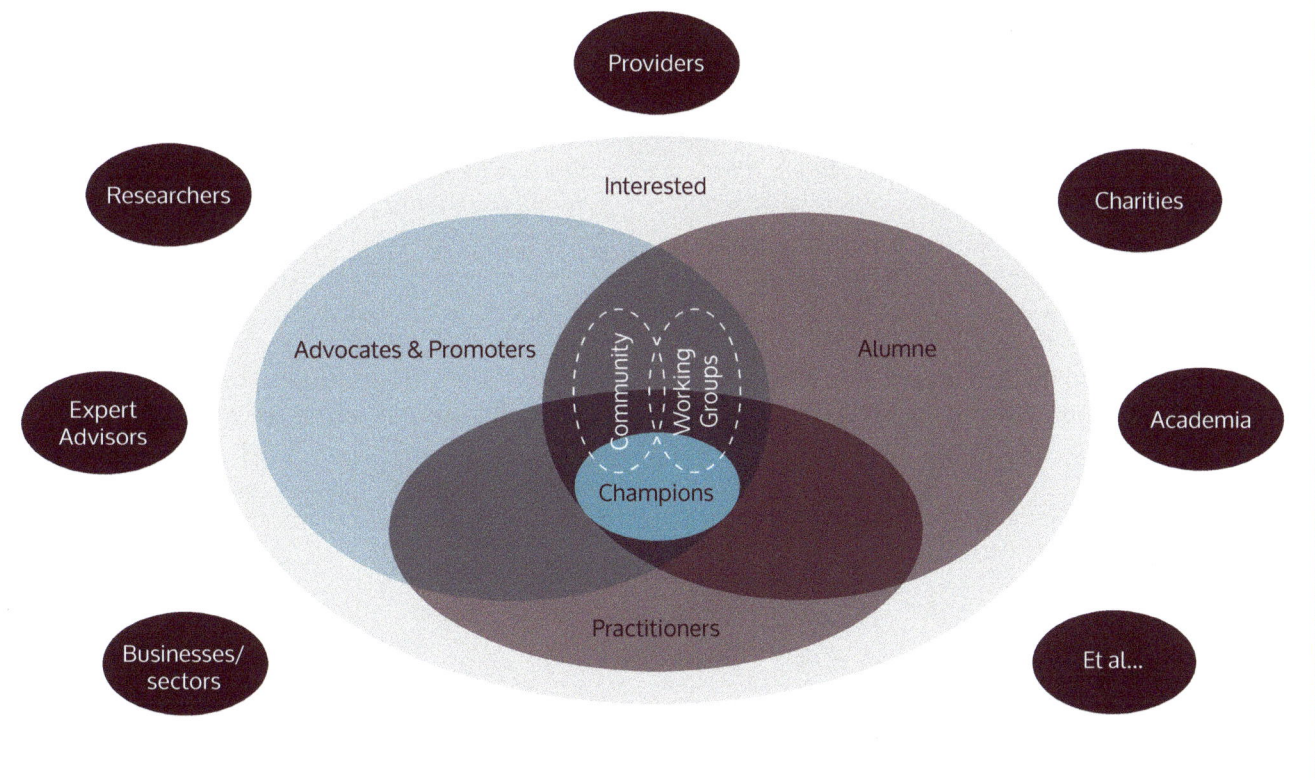

2.5
Establishing credibility

For beginners wanting to learn mindfulness practices, it can be hard to decide who to trust. As an innovator, what could give you the most credibility in earning this valuable trust? Depending on the nature of your innovation you will want to ensure that you and your team can collectively demonstrate the right experience and qualifications for the job.

Depth of personal practice

Innovators in the mindfulness space are likely to have deeply benefited from their own personal practice. This is usually the inspiration that drives people to find ways to share the benefits of mindfulness with others in a meaningful way. However, it is generally thought that decades of personal practice are needed before being able to skillfully develop an innovative new approach. One of the dangers of moving from just a short-term practice to an innovation is that the deeper transformational potential of the practice may be missed.

Instead of the years required to develop further mindfulness expertise themselves, some innovators may prefer to bring a 'content expert' on to their team. This is no different to bringing in other types of experts, for example if your innovation requires knowledge about how the prison systems operate, or the psychology of young children. For mindfulness expertise you may consider working with an experienced mindfulness practitioner or teacher. This person, or group of people, could be invited into your team as partners, employees, advisors, mentors or board members.

Whichever route you take, it is critical that your innovation is informed by depth of experience. After all, we don't know what we don't know! Advisors can help shed light on blind spots.

> **Tool box**
> ### Where to find experienced mindfulness practitioners
>
> In the UK, teacher-training for most mindfulness courses includes supervision by very experienced mindfulness teachers. Networks of supervisors could be an excellent source of expertise if you wish to employ an adviser for your innovation. For example, they will be able to guide you on which aspects of mindfulness teachings might be most relevant for your particular offering. They may also offer you support and mentoring to deepen your own practice as you go about developing your innovation.
>
> **The mindfulness network**
> www.mindfulness-supervision.org.uk/
>
> **Breathworks supervisor network**
> www.breathworks-mindfulness.org.uk/supervision
>
> A number of centres in the US and Canada focus on professional training for mindfulness-based programs and are connected with many mindfulness professionals. Prominent centres include: The Center for Mindfulness – UMass Medical School / UCLA Mindful Awareness Research Center / UCSD Center for Mindfulness / Mindfulness Center at Brown University / The Penn Program for Mindfulness / Centre for Mindfulness Studies, Toronto / Centre for Mindfulness Studies, Montreal / Mindspace, Montreal

> **We usually recommend people to be fully trained and then to teach the programme at least nine times before taking steps to adapt it."**
>
> – *Professor Mark Williams, Oxford Mindfulness Centre, co-creator of the MBCT programme*

Teaching experience

Training as a mindfulness teacher yourself can support your knowledge and credibility. In particular, if you intend to creatively adapt or improve a specific established programme without collaborating with expert teachers, you should first train in teaching the original curriculum and get some experience in delivering it. For example, MBSR, MBCT, Breathworks and other courses such as .b for schools, or Mindful Self-Compassion all have their own carefully designed teacher-training programmes. Such training can be a substantive investment in time and resources, taking between several months and several years to complete – but the process will deepen your understanding, inform your innovation and provide you with a support network of mindfulness practitioners and mentors.

There is currently no regulatory body overseeing mindfulness-based teaching anywhere in the world. However in some countries there are voluntary groups and associations working towards good practice guidance that maintain a listing of recognised teachers. In the UK this entity is known as the British Association of Mindfulness-based Approaches (BAMBA - formerly, the UK Network of Mindfulness-based Teacher Training Organisations). It represents the leading teacher training organisations in the UK committed to supporting and developing good practice and integrity in the delivery of mindfulness-based approaches.

In the US and Canada, no single body sets and maintains standards for all mindfulness teaching. Teachers of MBSR and MBCT usually turn to the organisations where they were trained for guidance and support. Mindfulness teachers outside of those programs have no unified standards organisation, although the International Mindfulness Teachers Association is working to fill this void. For a report on standardisation efforts in the US and Canada visit: www.mindful.org/how-to-find-an-authentic-mindfulness-teacher/

Explore further
Good practice networks

In some countries there are voluntary groups and associations working towards good practice guidance that maintain a listing of recognised teachers.

United Kingdom
bamba.org.uk

Germany
www.mbsr-verband.de/verband/ueber-uns.html

Netherlands
www.vmbn.nl/

Europe-wide
www.eamba.net/

US, Canada and International
There are no country-wide standards organisations or members associations in Canada or the USA. There are however some relevant international listings:

For MBSR, The Center for Mindfulness at UMass Medical School maintains a searchable listing of CFM-Certified teachers. www.umassmed.edu/cfm/mindfulness-based-programs/mbsr-courses/find-an-mbsr-program/

For MBCT, Access MBCT maintains a searchable listing of teachers who meet minimum requirements and a list of MBCT training programs worldwide. www.accessmbct.com/

The California-based International Mindfulness Teachers Association, formed in 2018, maintains a searchable directory of mindfulness teacher-training offered by member organisations that have met the association's criteria. www.imta.org/page/programdirectory

Aligning yourself with good practice standards

The BAMBA teachers listing sets high standards, requiring teachers to obtain independent verification by their supervisor as well as a referee from within the network. Teachers are also required to submit annual reports of their engagement with and commitment to the Good Practice Guidelines which emphasise ongoing practice, learning and development (see box).

If you are a mindfulness teacher you may want to join the relevant association in your country and commit to the good practice guidelines it promotes. If you are not a teacher then you can choose to work with teachers who have committed to such guidelines.

The Center for Mindfulness at UMASS Medical School has published MBSR Standards for Practice. This document includes a set of key principles and aspects of MBSR considered universally important in any teaching context. www.umassmed.edu/zzz/cfm/mindfulness-based-programs/mbsr-courses/about-mbsr/mbsr-standards-of-practice/

Having your course formally recognised

Looking ahead, you may apply for your innovative new course and its teachers to be recognised by an independent umbrella organisation to lend credibility and assurance about its safety and effectiveness. For example, in the UK, BAMBA recognises programmes through a process based on the "What Defines Mindfulness-Based Programs" paper as described at the end of Chapter 1. This process of approving new programmes is overseen by an independent panel of advisors. Over the past four years, six new mindfulness training courses have gone through this process and been added to their list, and this will continue to grow as new programmes are developed.

Ethical code of conduct

Thinking about and creating a code of conduct for yourself and your innovation can provide internal clarity as well as external credibility. As a reference, BAMBA has developed a code of conduct that highlights the following points:

- Respect for participants, no discrimination
- Communication with integrity and honesty

Tool box
Good Practice Guidelines for mindfulness teachers in the UK

All teachers of mindfulness-based courses should be able to demonstrate the following:

- Participation in the mindfulness-based course that you will teach

- Completion of an in-depth, rigorous teacher training programme or supervised pathway over a minimum of one year

- Professional qualification in mental or physical health care, education or social care, or equivalent life experience, depending on context

- Knowledge and experience of the population that the mindfulness-based course will be delivered to

- Commitment to a personal mindfulness practice through daily formal and informal practice, and participation in annual residential teacher-led retreats

- Engagement in processes (learning, supervision, inquiry) that continue to develop mindfulness-based teaching practice

- A commitment to ongoing development as a teacher through further training, keeping up to date with the evidence base etc

- Adherence to the ethical framework appropriate to the teacher's professional background and working context

Full document
bamba.org.uk/teachers/good-practice-guidelines/

- Adhering to the Good Practice Guidelines
- Taking steps to manage risk
- Respecting confidentiality

Full document bamba.org.uk/the-standards/

> **Innovation is needed to keep the mindfulness field relevant to the societies and communities it serves, and it is equally important for this to happen alongside recognised standards for safe, ethical and inclusive practices."**

- BAMBA Trustee Board (bamba.org.uk)

2.6 Business models

Why is a business model important?

Everyone needs to pay the bills - and financial viability is crucial for you as an innovator. Without an income stream you may not be able to put in the necessary time and resources to work productively on your innovation. Financial viability also allows you to grow your team, bringing with it diversity of perspectives, a more resilient and sustainable offering, and ultimately higher positive impact for users.

For the user, your financial viability helps ensure the quality and continuity of service. It also makes it easier for you to focus on serving those to whom the innovation is best suited, rather than needing to offer it to a different or wider group primarily for financial reasons. Being in a position to say "no" to users for whom your offering is not suited enables more ethical decision-making.

A well thought-out business model isn't at odds with prioritising positive social impact. Most innovations have multiple objectives. For example you may wish to reduce suffering, spread happiness, and create a profitable business. It is worth exploring which different objectives support one another, and where they may clash.

Stakeholder objectives

A core question in determining any business model is "who will pay?". It may be the participant or the end-user, but it might also be a local authority, school, university, employer etc.

Where the paying customer is a different entity from the participants actually learning mindfulness skills, there will be areas of alignment (where the interests of both are the same) but there may also be areas of difference. For example, a business customer may see "higher retention of employees" as one of the objectives of an in-house corporate mindfulness offering, whereas learning mindfulness may give some employees the awareness and insight that it would be healthier for them to leave the company.

Participant retention

Retention of participants in your programme is vital not only for financial viability but in most cases also for effectiveness: learning mindfulness practices takes time. Retention can become a problem when the participant does not pay for the product; behavioural observations suggest that when the end-user does not pay for a product or service their motivation for engagement is lower, making them more likely to drop out. One potential solution is to charge a small nominal payment.

Incentives such as credibility, acknowledgement and peer support may also help keep users engaged. The skills of the teacher are also important in building and sustaining motivation and momentum throughout the course.

Payment by voluntary donation

Inviting participants to make voluntary payments or donations for the course comes with both benefits and risks. Some consider it a market failure with the potential to leave service providers such as mindfulness teachers under-remunerated and burnt out. This makes the product or service delivery unsustainable in the longer-term.

Others note that keeping an offering financially open and flexible is valuable because it makes mindfulness accessible to a much wider group of people, as well as communicating a spirit of compassion and kindness which is itself part of the teaching.

It has also been observed that people who attend such donation-based courses can appreciate them more. Because teaching is not primarily based on a financial transaction it can feel more like a gift. Less concerned about 'value for money', a participant may feel inspired to share this gift with others or 'pay it forward' in some way.

Hybrid models

'Giving back' is a core part of some existing business models in mindfulness innovation, allowing some of the revenues to flow back to more vulnerable parts of the community that might not otherwise be able to participate. These include profit-making businesses with a charitable arm and social enterprises using legal entities such as Community Interest Companies (CICs).

Subscription models

In the digital space, subscription models are beneficial because they remove reliance on advertising revenue; helping to create a more focused and positive user experience in turn. Subscription commitments can also help create longer-term relationships and momentum, and build positive habits.

A subscription-based business model however contains an inherent incentive for acquisition and retention. For this model to succeed users must remain loyal and pay their monthly fees. Some argue that mindfulness should be taught in such a way that the user learns and becomes independent in their practice, perhaps no longer needing the subscription to a service. In trying to retain users we may end up creating a dependency, which does not necessarily serve the user's interest in the long-term.

Social investors and funders

Investors may be essential to your work, especially if you intend to scale your offering. They share your risk, financially and emotionally. Investors play a large role in defining metrics for success, and can have a strong influence on the way the innovation unfolds. The ideal investors are therefore those who resonate with your mission and whose values align strongly with the ethos of your innovation.

Social investors have boosted innovation in many societal, community and environmental spheres, because they care about the intended social impact as well as the financial health of the organisation. The size of the social investment market in mindfulness is currently very limited, with many of the existing mindful apps being funded by commercial tech investors.

Case study
iBme: Balancing financial sustainability with accessibility

iBme runs 5-day intensive mindfulness retreats for teenagers. A rigorous screening process involves a conversation with every applicant to ensure the retreat is a good fit for them. If a teenager is accepted then parents pay their fees. Retreats are expensive and the organisation has been keen to try and cover their costs directly from parents as much as possible. At the same time they didn't want anyone to be turned away for lack of funds. After several iterations of payment models they believe they have now struck a good balance.

How the iBme payment model has evolved:

- **Version 1.** Fixed fee or funded scholarship. This felt too binary, lacking options in between.

- **Version 2.** Flexible fee – "you choose" based on what you can afford. This was left open to interpretation and based on trust, with the result that families often paid the minimum amount only and the funding gap was substantial.

- **Version 3.** Radical sliding scale from 0 to $2000 per teenager. The family is asked to pay 1% of their income, up to a maximum of $2000. This is still based on a trust model but is much more directive. No applicant who is accepted is turned away for lack of funds. The gap is filled by a scholarship fund which is based on donations from funders.

Learn more about iBme's model:
www.ibme.info

Innovation landscape

Tool box
Business Model Canvas

A practical and comprehensive way to explore your business model is the Business Model Canvas. This simple sheet asks you key questions such as what your revenue stream will be, what resources are vital to your operation, and what key partnerships you will need to forge. Download and print out a Business Model Canvas and work with your team to fill it out. You may need to pause the process to gather more information as you progress.

Original version:
strategyzer.com/canvas/business-model-canvas

Social business adaptations, such as this one, might be more relevant:
www.socialbusinessmodelcanvas.com/

Key Resource	Key Activities	Type of Intervention	Segments	Value Proposition
				Beneficiary Value Proposi-
				Impact Measure
What resources will you need to run your activities? People finance, access?		What is the format of your intervention? Is it a workshop? A service? A product?	Who benefits from your intervention? Beneficiary Customer	
Partners + Key Stakeholders		**Channels**		
				Customer Value Proposi-
Who are the essential groups you will need to involve to deliver your programme? Do you need special access or permission	What programme and non-programme activities will your organisation be carrying out?	How are you reaching your users and custom-	Who are the people or organisations who will pay	What do your customers want to get out of this initiative?

Cost Structure		Surplus	Revenue	
What are your biggest expenditure areas? How do they change as you scale up?		Where do you plan to invest your profits	Break down your revenue sources by $	

Chapter 3

Designing with and for people

3.1 A human-centred approach

Designing with and for people

Innovation starts with a problem that people are facing and ends with a new kind of solution that meets their needs. By staying grounded in the experience of the people you wish to serve, you are more likely to come up with a solution that genuinely meets their needs, as well as creating champions and advocates for your approach.

The people you serve may be described as "end-users", "users", "participants", "target audience", "beneficiaries" or "affected communities" - each term has its own history and advantages. We use them interchangeably in this document. The lowest common denominator is that they are human beings.

Whatever you choose to call your group, it is important to recognise that they are the experts about their own culture, experiences, challenges and needs. The best way to learn about them is therefore to engage with them directly.

This approach is widely known as a human-centred or user-centric approach to innovation. In academia and especially public health it is known more as a participatory approach to research and development. Essentially these are all ways of keeping people at the centre of the innovation process at every stage, with an emphasis on genuine dialogue and close observation.

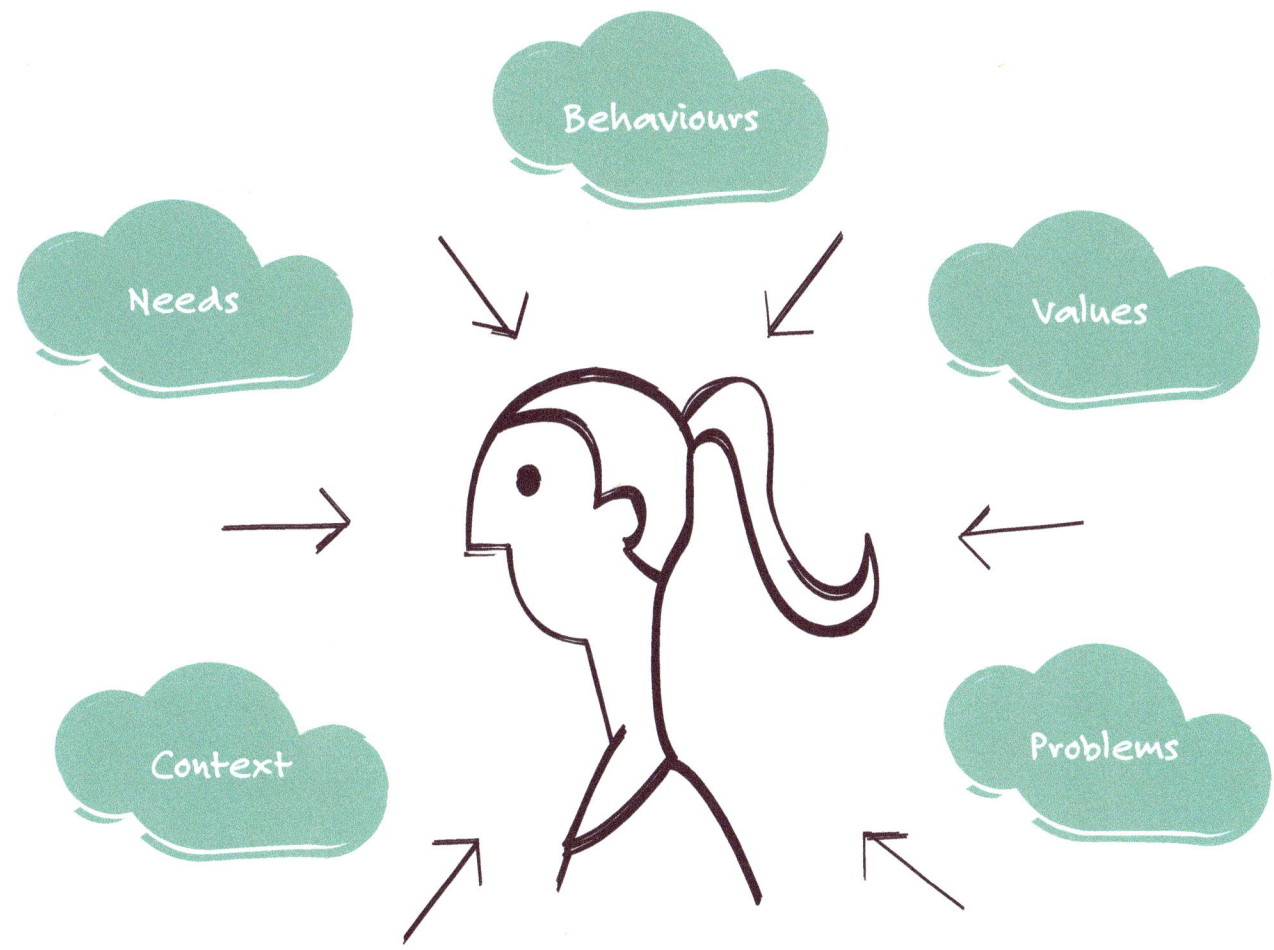

3.2 Starting with the problem

> **A problem well stated is a problem half-solved."**
>
> – Charles Kettering, inventor

It's often said of innovators that we tend to bend (or even invent) problems to fit a solution that we already have in mind. As the old saying goes "when all you have is a hammer, everything starts to look like a nail!" It's only natural that if we have a passion for mindfulness training, we will see potential benefits to its application in many different contexts. The best way to overcome this bias is to research the problem thoroughly, before approaching solutions.

Even if this problem is one close to your heart, or that you are intimately familiar with through personal experience, it is still important to take a step back and do the necessary research to check that your assumptions are correct.

The following questions may help you gain clarity:

- What problem are you trying to solve?
- What makes this problem important to you?
- What evidence do you have that this is really a problem?
- Who is this a problem for?
- In what context is this a problem?
- What assumptions are you making at this stage?
- What change or impact would you like to create?

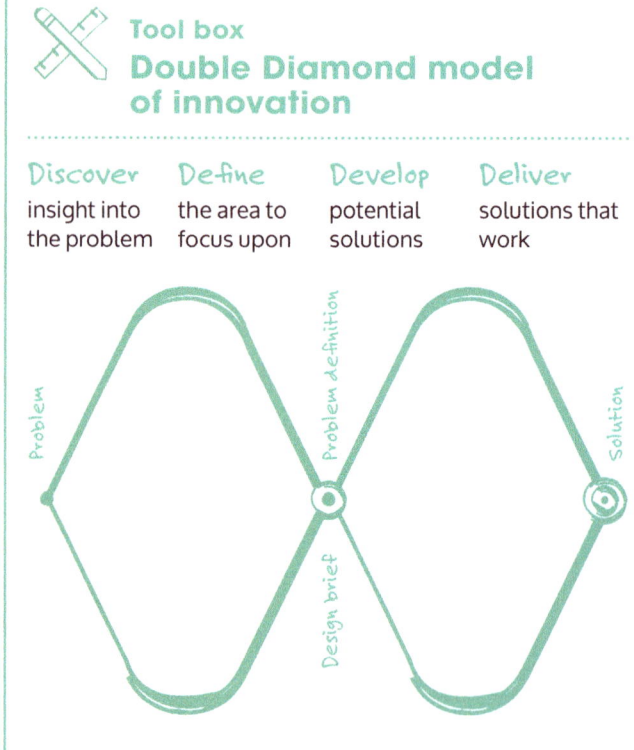

Tool box
Double Diamond model of innovation

Discover insight into the problem

Define the area to focus upon

Develop potential solutions

Deliver solutions that work

Source: Design Council UK www.designcouncil.org.uk/

This popular model offers a simple visual map that makes two important points. Firstly, that all creative processes involve both divergent thinking (exploring and expanding knowledge and ideas) and convergent thinking (refining and narrowing down). Secondly, that this cycle must happen at least twice: once to understand the problem, and again to solve it. One of innovation's greatest mistakes is to omit the left-hand diamond and end up solving the wrong problem!

Direct contact

Engaging your target audience directly through interviews and surveys will be an important part of this initial research into the problem. When planning this engagement consider the broadest spectrum of people whose lives your innovation will touch, not just the most common type of user.

Consider collaborating with local community facilitators that your target audience is already familiar with. This can help build trust more quickly, as well as avoiding potential insensitivity around triggers that you may not be aware of. On the other hand, sometimes a fresh outsider expressing genuine interest can elicit more reflective and candid responses.

Tool box
Guidance for interviews

In the early stages of exploration, the purpose of interviews is to understand the problem from the perspective of those experiencing it. Even if you are familiar with the problem, the ideal mindset is one of open-minded curiosity. This can be challenging, especially if you already have ideas about what kind of solution could work.

- Where possible, conduct the interview in the interviewee's space so that they are comfortable and can be themselves.

- No more than two or three team members should attend a single interview, so as not to overwhelm the participant. Each of you should have a clear role and introduce yourself accordingly (eg. interviewer, note-taker, photographer).

- Come with a set of questions you'd like to ask, making sure to balance both broad and specific questions.

- It helps to be specific — for example instead of asking participants to describe a 'typical day', ask them what they actually did yesterday.

- Write down the words they use, not your interpretation (you can reflect on this later). As far as possible, capture direct quotes - not a summary.

- For a different perspective, ask participants to explain their activities and experiences through diagrams.

- If appropriate, consider asking the participant for a guided tour through their environment as this can reveal their habits and values, sometimes more so than other questions.

Further creative prompts
Conversation starters
www.designkit.org/methods/44

Card sort
www.designkit.org/methods/24

Question ladder
diytoolkit.org/tools/question-ladder/

Designing with and for people

Arriving at a statement of the problem

A problem statement is a single statement that represents the nature of the problem, who is experiencing it, and why solving it is important. Articulating this carefully can focus your efforts, and make it easier for you to communicate what you are doing to a wider group of stakeholders.

Your framing of the problem should remain human-centred, which means focusing on the needs of the user group, rather than, for example, a method, technology or delivery model. Asking "How might we support children to use mindfulness of breath to experience less stress during exam time?" is more human-centred than "How might we adapt breath awareness techniques to be suitable for children?" which emphasises a method.

An ideal problem statement is broad enough to invite multiple possible solutions, and narrow enough to be focused and manageable. For example "How might we improve global levels of happiness?" is too broad a question to develop ideas around. At the other extreme, a long list of detailed technical requirements can swamp creativity.

Several iterations and refinements will usually be required to get it just right.

Tool box
Asking the right question

Framing your problem statement as a question can make it more inviting and provocative. Design thinkers recommend the "How might we..." question because 'how' keeps the focus on a practical solution, 'might' emphasises the possibility of more than one solution, and 'we' brings in the notion of collaboration.

Here is a template that you could use, inspired by the innovation agency IDEO.org:

How might we _____ ?

"How might we [human-oriented problem to solve] through/by [your hunch about the innovation needed] so that [important outcome that will happen.]"?

A properly framed question doesn't suggest a particular solution, but gives you the perfect frame for innovative thinking.

More guidance:
www.designkit.org/methods/3

Designing with and for people

Wider causes

Having honed in on a specific problem, it can be a powerful practice to 'zoom out' and consider causes beyond the immediate or obvious. For example, when considering depression, what is the role of diet and exercise? Wider causes might be linked to other parts of the system, some balancing each other out and others reinforcing each other in feedback loops.

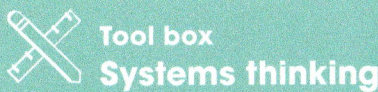

Tool box
Systems thinking

Analysis of causes, effects and the interactions between them is known as systems thinking. By employing systems thinking, as part of your problem analysis, you will be able to identify leverage points, which may enable you to be more efficient and create a bigger impact.

Tool for identifying causes
diytoolkit.org/tools/causes-diagram/

What is systems thinking?
www.youtube.com/watch?time_continue=10&v=GPW0j2Bo_eY

Systems thinking principles
www.disruptdesign.co/blog/2017/8/18/11-key-principles-of-systems-thinking

5 whys
www.designkit.org/methods/66

Recommended reading
Thinking in Systems: A primer. By Donella Meadows

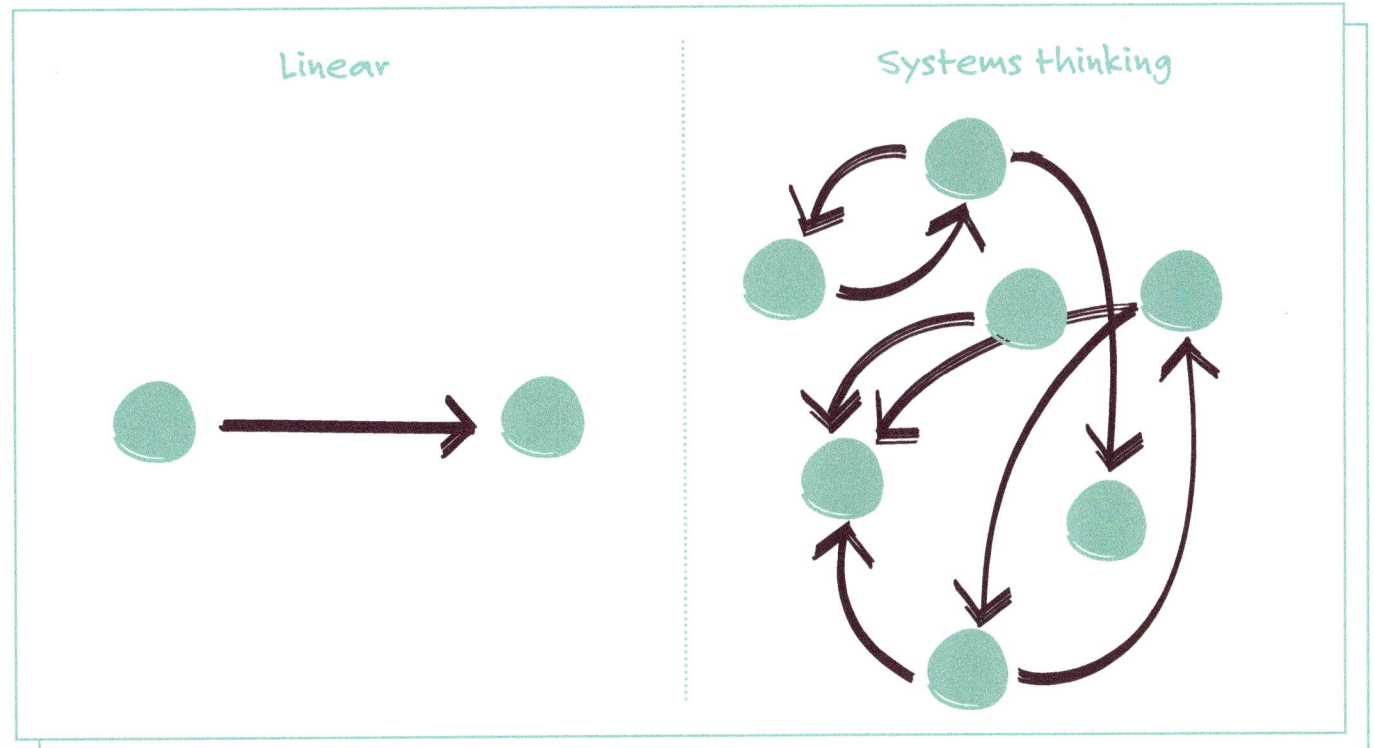

The Mindfulness Initiative / Fieldbook for Mindfulness Innovators

Reviewing existing theory and evidence about the problem

It's likely that for most problems you might aim to solve, significant theory and evidence already exists. Draw upon this resource to understand the issues from different perspectives. For example, if your focus is on supporting young people to reduce reoffending, you may wish to explore existing research and theories relating to the causes of this behaviour, especially its psychological drivers and triggers. All such insights would help you to identify how mindfulness might help.

As ever, keep in mind the cognitive bias that can lead you to reinforce your assumptions. Review the existing theories and evidence with an open mind.

Case study
MBCT: Analysis of the target problem and how mindfulness works

In the context of depression recurrence, the groundwork for the mindfulness programme known as MBCT was based on analysis of research and theory. Innovators asked the question "Why are those people who have experienced depression once more vulnerable to depression than others?". The innovators in this case were researchers so they conducted lab experiments (mood inductions) to understand what factors created mood changes and based on this they developed some theories. They believed that the skill needed to prevent recurrence of depression is to get people to 'de-centre' and see their thoughts. Initially they thought this could be achieved through a CBT (cognitive behavioural therapy) approach with a little bit of mindfulness mixed in. They soon realised that just a little bit of mindfulness wasn't enough, because participants stayed immersed in their thoughts and struggled to see them in perspective. People must be grounded more deeply in mindfulness for it to become a new way of being, allowing them to step back from thoughts.

Mapping out (1) how depression recurs, (2) the potential changes mindfulness offers, and (3) how the two can meet each other smoothly was an endeavour that took the creators of MBCT 30 years.

> **For mindfulness interventions to be successful it is necessary for practitioners to have a clear formulation of the disorder being treated and how a mindfulness intervention may be helpful for that disorder. We further believe that understanding mechanisms of change is necessary for a problem formulation approach to the use of mindfulness interventions"**
>
> Teasdale, J.D., Segal, Z., Williams,, J. M.G., (2003) Mindfulness Training and Problem Formulation, Clinical Psychology: Science and Practice, 10:157–160)

3.3 Co-creating a solution

Designing with and for people

Collaborating with participants

As you gain clarity on the problem and move into solution mode, complex questions about mindfulness practices, technology, delivery styles and business models can take over: it is easy to lose focus on the people that your innovation is intended to serve.

During this time, continuing conversations with people who are directly affected by the problem you are working on will feed you with ideas, insights and practical feedback as well as building a sense of co-ownership and excitement with the participants who will be testing the solution.

Tool box
Personas

A common method for understanding relevance is to build personas and stories which typify the people you are working for. A persona is a fictional but realistic representation of the needs, aspirations and goals of a target user. This is a way of making sense of the research you have already gathered. The benefit of having multiple stories is that you don't need to generalise all the users, but can highlight different types of users and their different needs. This process also helps build empathy with people who might be very different to you.

Importantly, named personas can provide a common reference point for discussion with your team or other stakeholders, reducing assumptions and creating alignment. When you get stuck in an internal debate you can ask, for example, "How is this relevant to 'Tina'?".

You may end up with around 5-10 personas. Each one should have a slightly different emphasis, and not be too similar.

Include for example:

- Name (fictional)
- Age, gender
- Family life
- Occupation
- Hobbies
- Likes / dislikes
- Daily routine
- Pain points (challenges)
- Motivations / aspirations

Adding an image and a quote that expresses the needs and goals of this type of user can help bring the persona to life.

Personas should be updated with your ongoing insights and may need to be discarded at some point. They are simply tools, which means discerning when it's appropriate to use them.

Resources for creating personas
opendesignkit.org/methods/personas/
diytoolkit.org/tools/personas/
diytoolkit.org/tools/storyworld/

Designing with and for people

A portfolio approach

As solutions start to take shape it is easy to become attached to favourite ideas - but in doing so you risk missing important possibilities. The portfolio approach is a strategic response to this risk, purposefully taking several ideas forward to the testing stage. Think of yourself as an investor with a portfolio of initial investments, hoping that multiple possibilities improve your chances of success.

Tool box
Brainstorming

The goal of a brainstorming session isn't one perfect idea, but rather lots of ideas! It is important to create an environment of "Yes, and…", rather than the "no, but…" which kills creativity. There will be plenty of time later to weed out unfeasible ideas. Right now the aim is to encourage wild ideas which could give rise to a creative leap.

Rules to set with the group:

- Defer judgement
- One conversation at a time
- Be visual
- Go for quantity
- Encourage wild ideas
- Build on the ideas of others
- Stay focussed on the topic

Learn more

Brainstorm rules
www.designkit.org/methods/28

Fast idea generator
diytoolkit.org/tools/fast-idea-generator/

Thinking hats
diytoolkit.org/tools/thinking-hats/

Understanding existing solutions

You are creating something new. However the problem you are trying to solve is unlikely to be new. How are people currently managing their situation and trying to meet their needs? What are the existing and emerging solutions, including those not based on mindfulness? Consider carefully the strengths and weaknesses of each alternative. This will give you clarity about the ways in which you hope that mindfulness training could help more effectively.

You may choose in this phase to be collaborative, and talk to as many people as possible already working in the same challenge area. It is particularly useful to find out what feedback and evaluation is available for existing solutions. This way you can build on the success of others and avoid repeating failures.

Choosing a delivery medium

In what ways will you deliver mindfulness teaching? In choosing a delivery medium it is important to explore issues around accessibility - for example affordability, attractiveness and social stigma. Each medium will entail compromise.

Virtual offerings that are delivered online or over the phone can be less safe and supportive than in-person teaching - but also more accessible in terms of affordability, geography and disability. Additionally, depending on personality and learning preferences, some people are more comfortable online than face-to-face or in a group.

You may consider introducing mindfulness practices to a small group of 'early adopters' in order to then discuss ideas such as different delivery mediums with them. One of the challenges at this stage of developing your offering is that participants may need some foundational experience of mindfulness to meaningfully co-create the solution with you.

Building a stakeholder map

Beyond your target group are other stakeholders, such as mindfulness teachers, funders and local authorities. You may even wish to collaborate with international stakeholders. Mapping them out early in the process helps you to keep them front of mind as you develop your innovation.

Tool box

This is a quick and simple way to visualise your community of stakeholders. Start by noting your target audience including beneficiaries, users or customers, and then work your way from the centre towards the outer layers, mapping other individuals and organisations that relate to your work. The closer to the core the more influential or important they are.

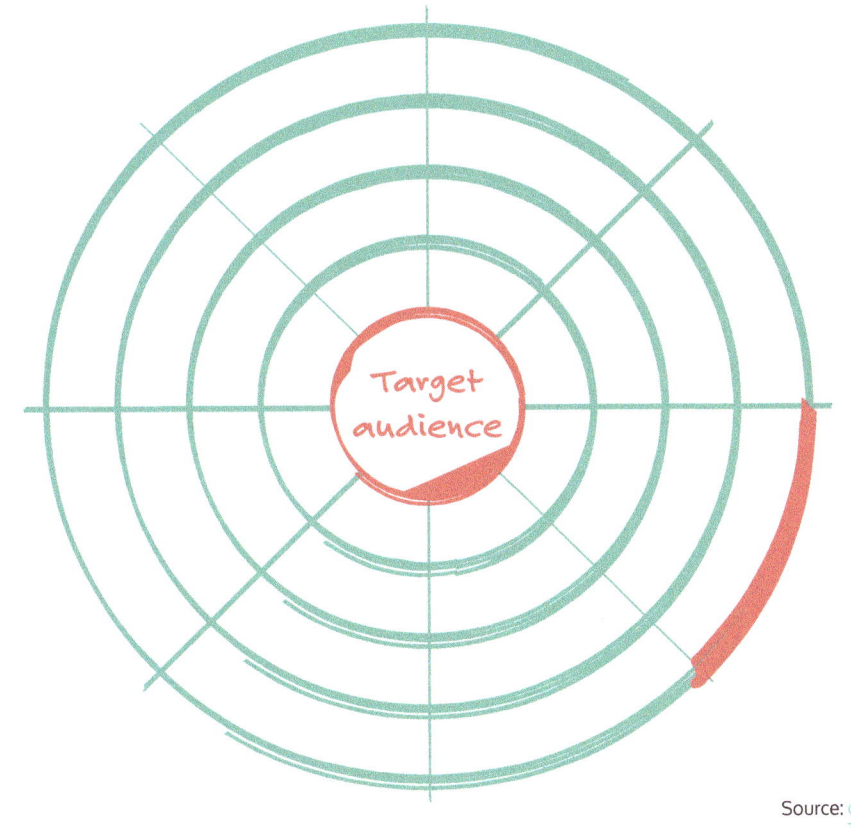

Organise stakeholders further by clustering them in sections that express specific networks, sectors or interest areas

Source: diytoolkit.org/tools/people-connections-map/

The Mindfulness Initiative / Fieldbook for Mindfulness Innovators

Case Study
Co-creating a Solution Iterating every element: Breathworks HEALS

Vidyamala Burch, the founder of Breathworks, has lived with spinal injury since 1976, and has been meditating since 1985 to work with her own mental responses to pain. Over time, she realised that it's not just mindfulness training that has helped, but also other related lifestyle factors such as nutrition, movement, sleep, relaxation, medication management, and connection with nature. She describes making "tiny changes in many different domains" in order to dramatically and sustainably improve one's quality of life. This insight led to the development of a new Mindfulness-based Lifestyle Medicine (MBLM) programme: HEALS (an acronym for Healthy Nutrition, Engaging with Movement, Awareness, Love and Sleep).

Each element of this new programme has been tested with the intended audience, collecting their direct feedback as well as using established psychological scales (e.g. for Anxiety, Depression, Quality of Life) to assess the impact the programme is having. This testing has informed a process of iteration. Some changes were major - for example, changing from a 6-week to a 10-week programme - while others were more subtle - for example, exchanging the term "exercise" for "engaging with movement" because many people with health conditions have a complex association with the word "exercise". Similarly, many people felt shamed by traditional sleep hygiene information and associated feelings of failure. The programme now includes a 'living document' where people share what has worked for them when addressing sleep issues due to pain and ill health, focusing on success and shared learning. All of these changes resulted from the collaborative approach.

3.4
Awareness of power dynamics

Designing with and for people

Risk of paternalism

Creating solutions to problems can sometimes create an unhealthy dichotomy of 'helper' and 'helped'. The mindset of helping may trigger misplaced responses such as pity or paternalism which may not be appreciated by the users of your product. Such oversimplified identities can create a barrier to deeper connection with your intended audience.

It can help to keep reminding ourselves that we all have needs, we all experience distress at times, and it just so happens that right now we have the opportunity to serve others.

>
> **Tool box**
> **The Little Book of Design Research Ethics**
>
> This guidance document emphasises the principles of respect, responsibility and honesty, considering the whole person and their context, with tangible examples of what this looks like in practice.
>
> Download the book
> lbodre.ideo.com/about/

Decentering authority: who defines benefit?

The more your target audience differs from you (in age, culture, language, values etc) the higher your risk of misunderstanding their needs. Where the innovation focuses on their suffering, it becomes especially easy to overlook the positive dimensions and possible richness of their lives.

In such contexts it is important that 'benefit', 'positive impact' and 'success' are all defined from the perspective of users. Innovators often mistakenly assume that their values and preferences are shared by their users. A more open, user-driven approach helps to ensure that you serve more than your own personal sense of what's right or needed.

This process of decentering can be much harder in practice than it seems - not least because of the expertise and special training that innovators usually have. Working to heighten our awareness and sensitivity to these issues is perhaps the best starting point.

> **Key Issue**
> **The danger of a single story**
>
> " The single story creates stereotypes and the problem with stereotypes is not that they are untrue but that they are incomplete. They make one story become the only story. The consequence of the single story is this: it robs people of dignity."
>
> Novelist Chimamanda Adichie warns that if we hear only a single story about another person or country, we risk a critical misunderstanding. Watch her TED talk www.ted.com/talks/chimamanda_adichie_the_danger_of_a_single_story

Designing with and for people

Not just "users" but complex human beings

Remember that the people you are working with are complex human beings and not only "users" of your solution. In the effort to keep things simple there is a risk of depersonalising the people you are working for. Data collection methods such as surveys can compound this tendency, in contrast to in-person interactions.

When conducting research on vulnerable groups, be aware of placing a large burden on their time. This time may be offered willingly (especially as the expectation is that the resulting solution will be being helpful) but it still comes at a cost to them.

When enquiring about personal challenges during the research phase, be aware that you risk stirring up difficult emotions in others that you may not be skilled or available to help manage in a healthy way.

Focusing on individuals can mask awareness of the fact that users belong to groups such as families and communities. From a solution perspective, accounting for the role of the group can help make or break a product or service.

3.5 Designing for a diverse society

Using secular language

To reflect today's diverse, secular society, you will likely want your innovation to appeal to people with all kinds of beliefs, including all faiths and none. This approach poses a specific set of challenges, especially if your own religious or philosophical belief system informs your approach.

While developing content it can be really hard to see the assumptions, beliefs and values implicit in your work - particularly in the language used. The resulting barriers might be small (for example, if users are unfamiliar with certain words) or highly significant (if for example groups are implicitly excluded, the ethics of the product may be called into question.)

Develop and test out language with those you want to serve. In particular, engaging with people outside of your own community of personal practice will help reveal what language genuinely feels inclusive. Inclusivity might entail avoiding faith-based references.

> **"Mindfulness principles are universal because they are about being present in whatever we do and can be used by people of any culture, or of any faith or none. I have been involved in presenting mindfulness to young Muslim imams in the Arab world and practicing it with them. In addition to the pleasure they take in mindfulness itself, they say it makes them more present to each other as well as in their recitations and rituals. 'Mindfulness helps us to pray better,' they say."**

– *Richard Reoch, Kalapa Leadership Academy*

For more information, see Richard's article: richardreoch.info/2016/12/09/absolutely-this-is-it/

If you feel strongly that faith associations in your programme or service are valuable for your desired impact, then it is important to be transparent by naming them. The critique of "religion through the backdoor" is avoided by being upfront about any faith-based influences.

A multi-faith approach can be an inclusive option. For example if you include a quote from the Buddhist tradition, you might also include quotes from Christian, Sufi and other traditions too.

Designing with and for people

Considering race, identity and culture,

Mindfulness training in its dominant forms is facing growing criticism for being insufficiently inclusive of and accessible to people of colour as well as those with other minority identities. The demographic of leading mindfulness institutions tends towards a white, middle-class profile among decision-makers and staff that is mirrored in its audiences and choice of training resources. For example, there is often a lack of diverse cultural representation in the poetry, imagery, videos, research and world wisdoms referenced. There is also a heightened awareness of the potential harm mindfulness teachers can do in the classroom when they are insufficiently socially or culturally aware. For example, group sharing with strangers is not necessarily a norm for certain communities, and sharing emotions outside of the family can be experienced as risky or even unethical behaviour. Participants may feel especially uncomfortable discussing external stressors such as racism, homophobia, male supremacy, etc. unless a sense of safety and trust has been built within the group.

In response, there is a growing movement to make mindfulness practice more accessible by supporting mindfulness teachers, researchers and innovators from within marginalised communities, as well as encouraging established institutions to adapt and diversify. The Sussex Mindfulness Centre, as a leading example, is working in partnership with Third Sector organisations to deliver culturally sensitive mindfulness programmes free of charge and tailored to communities they consider "underrepresented", such as BAPOC and LGBTQ+ populations.

Given the systemic nature of these problems, what can you personally do about this as a mindfulness innovator, whatever your background? If you're seeking to adapt and widen access within your own community, case studies such as Urban Mindfulness Foundation (see box on next page) can be supportive in demonstrating the compatibility of core mindfulness principles with different cultural traditions and the great potential for adaptations to enrich teaching and transform access.

If you're newer to conversations around diversity, to help make your innovation safer and more inclusive of diverse human experiences, you may want to consider some of the following books and resources as a starting point. (see box below). As you develop your offering, ask yourself how you might respectfully consult and include people with lived experiences different to your own, especially if that means those from marginalised communities, to better understand what they need from an inclusive mindfulness learning space.

Explore further
Resources to bring issues of race, identity and culture into mindfulness training

Awakening Together: The Spiritual Practice of Inclusivity and Community, Yang, L. (2017), Wisdom Publications

Disrupting White Mindfulness: Race and Racism in the Wellbeing Industry, Karelse, Cathy-Mae (2023), Manchester University

Mindfulness-Based Stress Reduction for Our Time: A Curriculum that is up to the Task. Crane RS, Callen-Davies R, Francis A, et al. *Global Advances in Integrative Medicine and Health.* 2023;12.

The Inner Work of Racial Justice: Healing Ourselves and Transforming our Communities Through Mindfulness, Magee, R.V. (2021), Tarcher Perigee,

Why I'm No Longer Talking to White People About Race. Eddo-Lodge, R. (2018), Bloomsbury publishing

Othering and Belonging Institute at the University of California Berkley belonging.berkeley.edu/

Designing with and for people

> ### Case Study
> ### Urban Mindfulness Foundation: Mindfulness Practice in Full Colour
>
> Dean and Aesha Francis both grew up in some of the most culturally diverse boroughs of London, where they faced the realities of relative poverty, social deprivation and identity-based harms such as racism and sexism, sometimes on a daily basis. Later in their lives, they came across mindfulness training as a different way of being that helped with these struggles and challenges. Both of them found the practice of mindfulness transformative and they went on to train as mindfulness teachers and study Mindfulness at the postgraduate level so that they could share this valuable resource with others more broadly and with greater depth. In particular, they wanted to share the practice with people from diverse backgrounds and identities, including African and Caribbean heritages.
>
> As they began sharing the mindfulness-based programme that they had trained to teach, they found that it lacked impact, and even risked harming some people in the room because it lacked cultural relevance and appropriateness.
>
> To address this problem, Dean and Aesha created the Urban Mindfulness Foundation to develop and provide mindfulness training programmes that are designed to be more inclusive. An underlying belief in their work is that mindfulness is an innate human capacity, and therefore a part of many ancient spiritual and religious traditions of the world, including Africa. In their training programmes, they explore concepts such as "Umoja", "Sankofa", "Ubuntu", and "Ubele" as part of their mindfulness guidance. They have found that doing this invites people to compassionately explore their own backgrounds and wisdom traditions as an authentic root into mindfulness that supports - rather than undermines - their sense of self-worth, belonging and or cultural heritage.
>
> Urban Mindfulness Foundation now offers a unique teacher training called Mindfulness-Based Inclusion Training (MBIT), which is delivered through a social justice, equity, diversity, and inclusion lens. They also support existing mindfulness teachers and organisations that want to be more culturally informed and sensitive in their classrooms.
>
> To learn more, visit:
> www.urbanmindfulnessfoundation.co.uk

> "Mindfulness and other wellness industries have a tendency to whitewash core concepts and practices. This stems from Othering, that emerged through years of colony and empire. Wealth and knowledge were extracted, repackaged, and then re-presented as universal and apolitical. This marginalises, racialises, harms and excludes people of the global majority. To correct these imbalances, the global majority need more representation, decision-making power, and platforms to voice different perspectives within White mindfulness spaces."

Cathy-Mae Karelse, author of Disrupting White Mindfulness: Race and Racism in the Wellbeing Industry

Cultivation of values

One of the benefits of mindfulness is that it helps individuals recognise what they truly value and find meaningful. As Professor Rebecca Crane, Director of the *UK Centre for Mindfulness Research and Practice*, observed, mindfulness training enables connection with personally held values such that individuals are "more empowered to make choices that align with these values". Some mindfulness programmes make use of this sensitivity to values in a therapeutic context. Among the most established of these is Acceptance & Commitment Therapy (ACT), a mindfulness-based approach that is used for a wide range of health issues, including eating disorders and chronic pain.

In addition to increasing sensitivity and alignment to values, mindfulness is often associated with pro-social or 'intrinsic' values such as care and compassion. Some studies have linked high mindfulness scores with more ethical decision-making and more environmentally responsible behaviour. Although there is some evidence that mindfulness training boosts these qualities even without teaching components specifically aimed at cultivating them, many experts believe that they should be more explicitly promoted as part of any course. One reason for doing so is that the cultivation of compassion has a mutually reinforcing relationship with other core outcomes such as attention regulation and acceptance, and can be a powerful enabler of practice.

Explore further
Ethics and values in Mindfulness

Baer, Ruth (2015) **Ethics, Values, Virtues, and Character Strengths in Mindfulness-Based Interventions: a Psychological Science Perspective.** Mindfulness (2015) 6: 956. doi.org/10.1007/s12671-015-0419-2

Bristow, J., Bell, R., Nixon, D. (2020). **Mindfulness: developing agency in urgent times. The Mindfulness Initiative.**
www.themindfulnessinitiative.org/agency-in-urgent-times/

Niemiec, Ryan & Lissing, Judith. (2016). **Mindfulness-Based Strengths Practice (MBSP) for Enhancing Well-Being, Managing Problems, and Boosting Positive Relationships.**
www.researchgate.net/publication/298351645_Mindfulness-Based_Strengths_Practice_MBSP_for_Enhancing_Well-Being_Managing_Problems_and_Boosting_Positive_Relationships

> **When practicing mindfulness, we bring an intention to cultivate an internal climate of friendliness towards all experience.**

– Professor Rebecca Crane, Director of the UK Centre for Mindfulness Research and Practice

Chapter 4

Does it work?

4.1 Why is evidence important?

Among innovators, a common critique of 'research and evidence' culture is that it can swamp the momentum and creative spirit that drives fresh perspectives, risk-taking and other ingredients of innovation. Mindfulness researchers and stewards of best practice meanwhile caution against unsubstantiated innovation based more upon good intentions than evidence, with the potential to do more harm than good.

Our aim here is to reduce any sense of conflicting priorities, explaining how innovation can be dynamic while remaining well-grounded and safe. As we will see, timing and appropriateness are key factors in deciding what kind of evidence to pursue.

> **Oxford English dictionary definition of evidence**
>
> "The available body of facts or information indicating whether a belief or proposition is true and valid."

What is evidence?

The term 'evidence' can name a wide spectrum - from qualitative feedback from users and teachers, through to results of randomised controlled trials (RCTs). What counts as "useful evidence" depends on its purpose, the question it is trying to answer, how it will be used, and in what environment. Commonly used (and misused) terms like 'impact', 'evidence-based' or simply 'what works' point to the basic good practice of trying to ascertain objectively the extent to which an intervention actually makes a difference.

> ❝ **We believed that our retreats were having a profound impact, based on the regular feedback from teens, parents and mentors (staff) that we spoke to, but independent research has given us hard evidence that others can take seriously too. This has been useful when building partnerships and raising funds. The research also helped us to validate some of our hypotheses about how our retreats are effective. For example, teens kept telling us that the retreats made them 'feel loved', 'feel accepted' and 'feel like I belong', and the study we took part in about mindfulness and self-compassion grounded that in science and gave us more confidence."**
>
> – Jessica Morey, Executive Director of iBme

Learn more about this mindfulness and self-compassion study in adolescents:
www.mindfulselfcompassionforteens.com/wp-content/uploads/2016/06/Galla-2016-teens-and-M-and-SC.pdf

Does it work?

Ten reasons to build your own evidence:

1. **Improving:**
   Testing and discovering the extent to which your intervention works opens up creative space for improvement.

2. **Safety and confidence:**
   If a product or service is going to interfere in people's lives, we should be confident that it is truly beneficial and at the very least causes no harm. Ensuring effectiveness also reduces the 'opportunity cost' – the benefit that the user would have received trying something more effective with their limited time, attention and resources.

3. **Contributing to the mindfulness community:**
   Sharing information about what works and what does not is a valuable contribution to the community, helping to build collective knowledge. It may also lead to unanticipated new collaborations.

4. **Building trust:**
   There are many ways to earn the trust of a user – being honest about results is an important factor.

5. **Credibility:**
   Published evidence is important to certain sectors and types of organisation in deciding to collaborate, commission or purchase your product or service. This includes most large organisations in the public and corporate sectors.

6. **Demonstrating value for money:**
   Proof of effectiveness can help your offering compete with differently priced alternatives – particularly important in contexts where funding is limited and the stakes are high, for example in schools. Evidence that allows a comparison with other options is fundamental to decision-making in such contexts.

7. **Sustaining projects in the long-term:**
   Particularly in large organisations, evidence is required to maintain funding for a programme in the budget after the business or policy context changes, a senior champion moves roles, or attention otherwise shifts to another area.

8. **Finding the right team:**
   As you grow your organisation, you will find it easier to attract talent to help build, champion and invest in your innovation if it has been proven independently to work.

9. **Raising funds:**
   Both public and private funders are more likely to support projects with stronger evidence. As social investors become more impact-focused they look to support projects that can generate a strong "social return on investment". Their investment decisions, often taken in stages, will be influenced by the level of testing and evidence that has been generated. Even small-scale pilot projects can encourage a funder to believe that your work is serious and credible.

10. **Influencing policy and practice:**
    Evidence is a powerful tool for influencing change and is one of the key features of effective policy-making. Evidence-based design has become increasingly established in the public sector.

4.2 Early testing and iteration

Does it work?

> **"Fail early, fail fast, fail forward"**
> – John C Maxwell, author of Fail Forward

The more time and resources we have invested in an idea, the less willing we might be to discard it when we discover its drawbacks. In both your own interest and that of the user, it is therefore essential to test your solution in the early phases of development, and use the feedback to improve your design before making costly investments. Early testing helps maximise learning from the beginning and allows you to discover whether the assumptions you have made about the way your intervention will work are valid.

A prototype is a model of your solution, like a draft. It is used to test and to obtain feedback which can influence improvements in design while iteration can be achieved rapidly and relatively cheaply. A prototype may be handled by users but will not be disseminated.

Source: Frits Ahlefeldt: fritsahlefeldt.com

Prototypes differ from pilots. Prototypes can be made at early stages and are experimental; their purpose is to learn as much as possible, as early as possible. Pilots are usually implemented later in the process, often as 'phase 1' of a roll-out, with a view to ironing out any final creases.

Key Issue
Build, measure and learn

A **minimum viable product (MVP)** is the simplest, cheapest, quickest version of your solution that can be built and delivered to the market in order to continue testing and learn about what works and what does not. Each time the product is improved it can be tested again. However each version of the product made for testing must be complete, rather than a small part of the overall solution. The purpose at this point is not necessarily to satisfy the user, but to learn.

Learn more:
theleanstartup.com/principles
diytoolkit.org/tools/improvement-triggers/

What is minimum viable product?

Not this

Like this

Does it work?

In-house experiments

Early-stage testing mostly involves simple comparison of the situation before and after your intervention (known as a 'pre- and post- test'), using mostly qualitative feedback. It is likely cost- and time-effective to design these tests yourself or with your team. Later when testing a more finished and operational solution, it may be worth partnering with an external research organisation or hiring specialised capacity in order to design a strong methodology for your experiments.

Deciding what to measure

> "Measure what you treasure"

– *Prof. Ruth Baer, Oxford Mindfulness Centre*

Data can be collected in so many different areas that deciding what to measure can be tricky. The advice from experienced researchers is to focus on outcome metrics relevant to your own essential objectives. For example, if you believe that your approach will improve confidence by increasing feelings of compassion, then find ways to measure levels of both compassion and confidence.

Your testing will be most valuable if you prioritise measuring outcomes over inputs, activities and outputs. For example if you want to improve the lives of young people with multiple support needs, it is not especially meaningful to record only the level of investment made, number of courses run and number of young people who turned up. You should rather find ways of measuring how and to what extent your intervention meaningfully improved their lives.

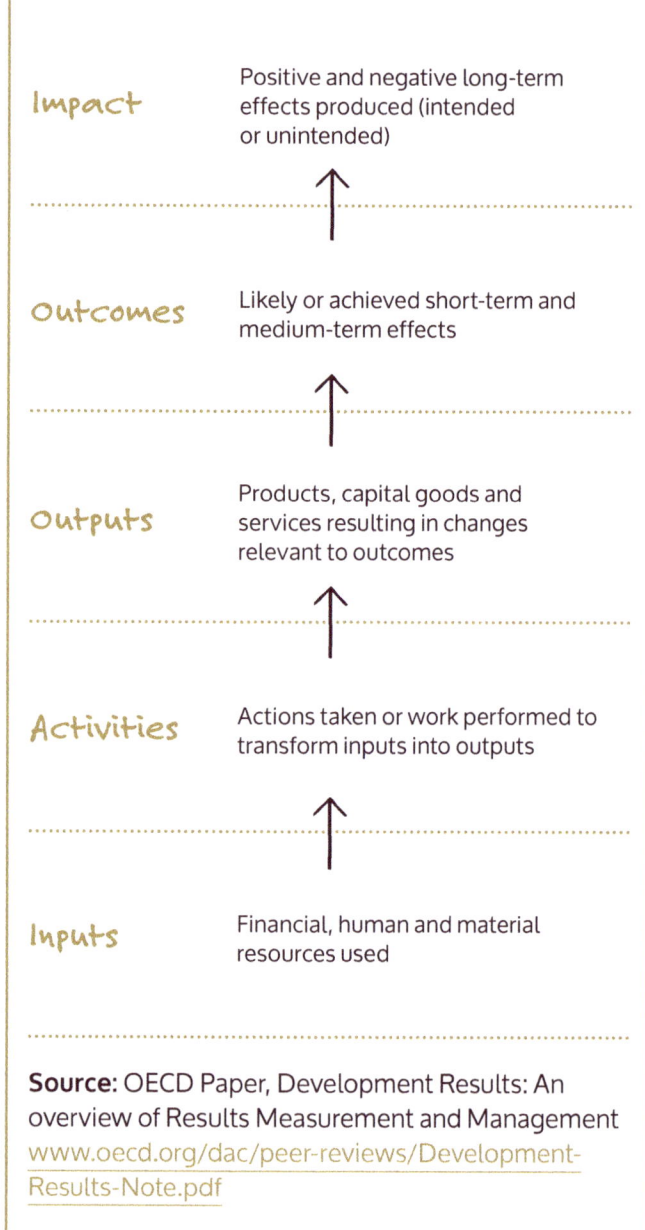

Impact: Positive and negative long-term effects produced (intended or unintended)

Outcomes: Likely or achieved short-term and medium-term effects

Outputs: Products, capital goods and services resulting in changes relevant to outcomes

Activities: Actions taken or work performed to transform inputs into outputs

Inputs: Financial, human and material resources used

Source: OECD Paper, Development Results: An overview of Results Measurement and Management
www.oecd.org/dac/peer-reviews/Development-Results-Note.pdf

Seeking accurate information

Human beings make sense of the world using cognitive shortcuts that are sometimes helpful, but at other times lead us to make mistakes. For example, most of us have an inbuilt tendency to favour information that fits with what we already believe: an error known as 'confirmation bias'.

Awareness of bias is especially important when assessing and developing an intervention that we are passionate about. For example, it's difficult to know whether the participants you've spoken to about the impact of your programme are representative of the entire group. Bias could lead us to assume so when they say complimentary things, and to seek a second opinion when they don't, producing inaccurate results.

Furthermore, those who do not complete the course or offer feedback may have had a negative experience that counter-weighs positive feedback offered by course completers. To obtain accurate reflections it is therefore important to actively measure diverse opinions, and to commit to gathering evidence systematically.

Results can be further confounded if participants who feel a need to please simply tell you what they think you want to hear. It is always best to engage an independent evaluator.

Another way of avoiding bias is to be open about the research steps you plan to carry out. For example, you can express in a public document your intention to use a particular scale to compare a participant group with a control group after a certain period of time. Committing to details such as these holds you to account, making it less likely that you will be tempted to change things as you go along in order to make your research outcomes appear more favourable.

Case-study
Mindfulness in Schools Project: Early days of feedback and evidence gathering

The Mindfulness in Schools Project's first product, the .b curriculum, was initially developed by three school teachers from different schools. They felt passionately that it was important to teach teenagers mindfulness skills and created a curriculum that they thought would work in classrooms, based on their experience both as mindfulness practitioners and school teachers.

The core principles of their work come from the eight-week MBCT and MBSR courses, but these required significant adaptation and reframing to be fit for purpose in a classroom context. Whenever they wondered if an adaptation might be too radical, they checked in with the creators of MBCT and MBSR for guidance. They then taught the programme to teenagers in their respective schools. After every class they compared notes and tweaked their materials repeatedly until they engaged pupils from start to finish.

mindfulnessinschools.org/

> "We were always getting feedback from the students, to find out what was working. It's pretty obvious when the kids are falling asleep or are bored, but you don't know where the boundaries and sensitivities are until you've tried teaching them. Trial and error has been fundamental to our approach – we are now in the 10th version. We are constantly adding lessons, improving parts, cutting out superfluous bits; we try to never be complacent."

– Richard Burnett, co-founder of the Mindfulness in Schools Project

Does it work?

Designing questionnaires using scales

Designing a questionnaire or survey to collect participant responses requires a lot of thought. There are many options for content and style (open, closed, multiple choice etc.). Established psychological scales can provide focus and direction, as well as making your results directly comparable with any existing initiatives measured using the same scale. Scales are sets of questions with scored answers that are designed to elicit honest responses, and home in on the most important aspects of the test.

Tool box
Psychological scales

Well-established and respected psychological scales that you might consider are listed below. Some of these scales will be more relevant to you and your stakeholders (including funders) than others. The mindfulness scales are not commonly used beyond the mindfulness world, and it may be more useful to show that your product or service improves e.g. stress or wellbeing rather than dispositional mindfulness. Note: For correct use of a scale, and for your results to be comparable to others using the same scales, the questions should not be altered in any way.

Mindful attention and awareness scale (15 questions)
Brown, K. W., & Ryan, R. M. (2003). The benefits of being present: Mindfulness and its role in psychological well-being. Journal of Personality and Social Psychology, 84(4), 822-848.

Five facets of mindfulness questionnaire (39 questions)
Baer, R. A., Smith, G. T., Hopkins, J., Krietemeyer, J., & Toney, L. (2006). Using self-report assessment methods to explore facets of mindfulness. Assessment, 13(1), 27-45.

ONS Personal Wellbeing scale (4 questions)
www.ons.gov.uk/peoplepopulationandcommunity/wellbeing/methodologies/surveysusingthe4officefornationalstatisticspersonalwellbeingquestions

Satisfaction with life scale (5 questions)
Diener, E., Emmons, R. A., Larsen, R. J., & Griffin, S. (1985). The satisfaction with life scale. Journal of Personality Assessment, 49(1), 71-75. doi: 10.1207/s15327752jpa4901_13

Positive and negative affect scale (20 questions)
Watson, D., Clark, L. A. C., & Tellegen, A. (1988). Development and validation of brief measures of positive and negative affect: The PANAS scales. Journal of Personality and Social Psychology, 54, 1063-1070. doi: 10.1037/0022-3514.54.6.1063

Self-compassion scale (12 questions)
Neff, K. D. (2003). The development and validation of a scale to measure self-compassion. Self and Identity, 2(3), 223-250.

Depression anxiety stress scale (42 questions)
Lovibond, P. F., & Lovibond, S. H. (1995). The structure of negative emotional states: Comparison of the Depression Anxiety Stress Scales (DASS) with the Beck Depression and Anxiety Inventories. Behaviour Research and Therapy, 33(3), 335-343. doi: dx.doi.org/10.1016/0005-7967(94)00075-U

Maslach burnout inventory (25 questions)
Maslach, C., Jackson, S., & Leiter, M. (1986). Maslach Burnout Inventory Manual. Palo Alto, CA: Consult. Psychol. Press.

Perceived stress scale (10 questions)
Cohen, S., Kamarck, T., & Mermelstein, R. (1983). A global measure of perceived stress. Journal of Health and Social Behavior, 385-396.

Social connectedness scale (8 questions)
Lee, R. M., & Robbins, S. B. (1995). Measuring belongingness: The Social Connectedness and the Social Assurance scales. Journal of Counseling Psychology, 42(2), 232-241. doi: 10.1037/0022-0167.42.2.232

The Warwick-Edinburgh Mental Wellbeing Scales (WEMWBS) (14 questions) warwick.ac.uk/fac/sci/med/research/platform/wemwbs/

Additional scales for "Evaluating an MBCT service"
www.implementing-mbct.com/2017/03/22/evaluating-an-mbct-service/

Risks of early testing

Ethical issues surround all stages of testing when working with vulnerable groups, and great care must be taken to avoid harm. Failure of the product or service in early testing may put the wellbeing of vulnerable participants at risk. On the other hand, testing early and on a small scale may help you avoid more significant and harmful failure at a later stage.

It can be necessary to measure harm actively: evidence from many fields shows that simply waiting for those who were harmed to come forward and tell you underestimates the problem and will miss many cases. Seek the opinions of those who stopped attending your course, and ask everyone who started the course to answer your post intervention questions.

The Economic and Social Research Council (ESRC)'s guidelines document contains further valuable suggestions: esrc.ukri.org/funding/guidance-for-applicants/research-ethics/frequently-raised-topics/research-with-potentially-vulnerable-people/

Similar guidelines produced by universities can be found online. If you work with a research group such as a university they will have ethical guidelines and ethics committees to provide oversight. It is advisable to engage mental health professionals to guide you on how to protect the people you are working with in your trials.

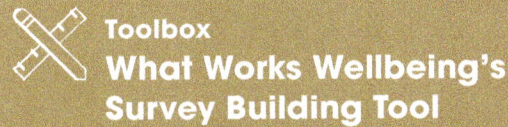

Toolbox
What Works Wellbeing's Survey Building Tool

The Community Interest Company **What Works Centre for Wellbeing** offers several practical resources online. 'How To Measure Your Impact on Wellbeing' includes a survey building tool, to help you put together a set of simple questions and to analyse results in a meaningful way.

measure.whatworkswellbeing.org

4.3 Explaining how your solution will work

Most likely you will already have ideas about how your innovation works. If your model has several elements it can be useful to break it down and lay out the assumptions and logic behind your thinking. This breakdown can be treated as a working hypothesis, which becomes the foundation of any testing and research.

Choosing a framework for your explanation

Theory of Change and **logic models** are two well established frameworks for mapping out your model. Both serve similar purposes, with differences in approach. A theory of change shows the messiness of the 'real world' and is often used to demonstrate long-term social impact, whereas a logic model homes in on a specific pathway within your solution, simplifying it in a way that makes it amenable for designing tests and experiments.

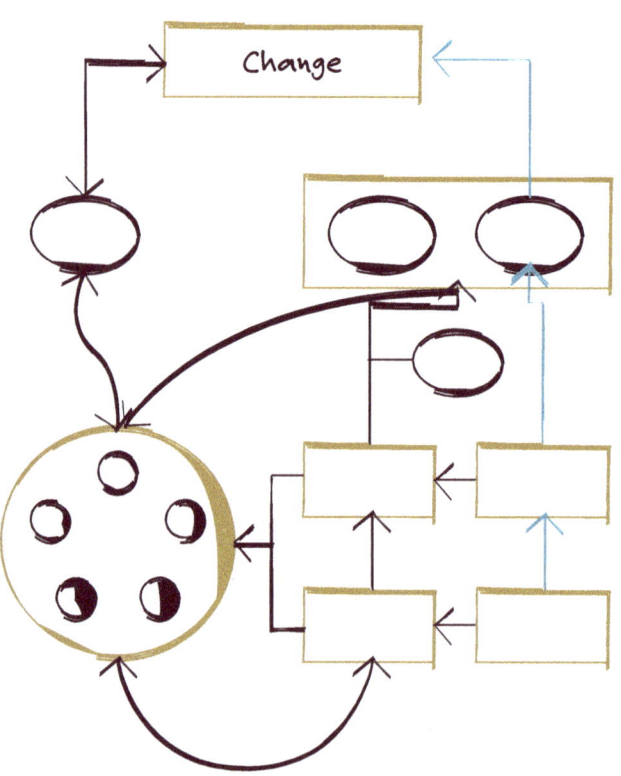

Theory of change
Shows the big picture with all possible pathways — messy and complex

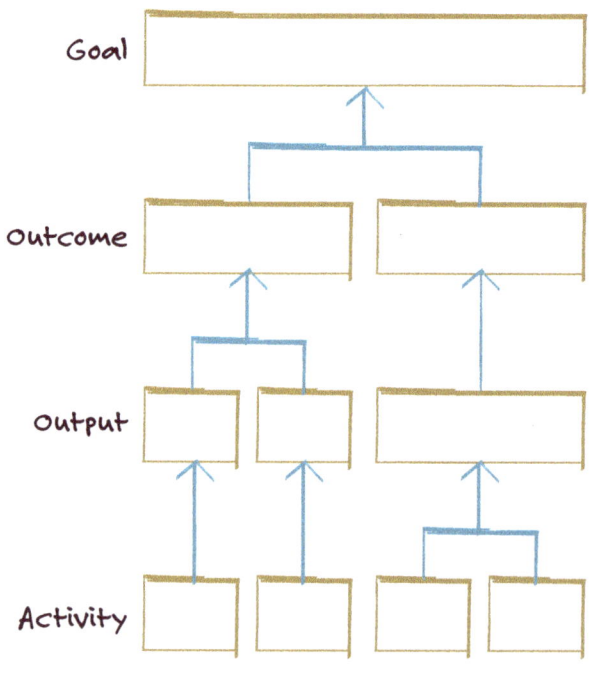

Logic Model
Shows just the pathway that your program deals with — neat and tidy

> **"Every programme is packed with beliefs, assumptions and hypotheses about how change happens – about the way humans work, or organisations, or political systems, or eco-systems. Theory of change is about articulating these many underlying assumptions about how change will happen in a programme."**

– Patricia Rogers, evaluation expert

Theory of change

While no single methodology defines a theory of change, the following would usually be included:

- Context of the initiative, including social, political and environmental conditions, the current state of the problem and other actors able to influence change

- Long-term change that the initiative seeks to support and identification of beneficiaries

- Process of change anticipated to produce the desired long-term outcome

- Assumptions about how these changes might happen

- Diagram and narrative summary capturing the desired outcomes

Source:
DFID review
assets.publishing.service.gov.uk/media/57a08a5ded915d3cfd00071a/DFID_ToC_Review_VogelV7.pdf

Theory of change resources
www.theoryofchange.org/library/publications/
diytoolkit.org/tools/theory-of-change/

Logic model

A logic model is a detailed description showing the relationship between inputs and specific outcomes. Any test of change will involve co-occurring factors, so it's important to be able to demonstrate causality and not just correlation.

Learn more about logic models:
www.annafreud.org/media/3498/ebpu-logic-model-200416final.pdf

"Logic model development guide" by W.K. Kellogg Foundation
www.wkkf.org/resource-directory/resource/2006/02/wk-kellogg-foundation-logic-model-development-guide

A brief overview of logic models (video):
www.youtube.com/watch?v=bZkwDSr__Us

4.4 Moving up the evidence hierarchy

> "To innovate in the current day and age, especially in the mindfulness space, to say 'It works for me' is not enough. We need to ask 'Is this the most impactful thing to put out there?' There needs to be patience and discipline in developing the idea. It is important to understand the mechanism of how mindfulness is working in our products, and what practices people are really benefiting from."
>
> – Dr. Jud Brewer, founder of Mindsciences.com

The term 'evidence' usually names a process of gathering information through research. This is in contrast to relying on expert advice, which can be misleading even when the individuals consulted are highly trained and have the best of intentions.

Research can include a wide range of methods – from stakeholder feedback and case studies through to ethnographic research and experimental studies. 'Evidence Hierarchies' rank these different evaluative methods according to their relative authority. For example, a pre- and post- test study might tell you if your group felt better after your intervention, but not whether your intervention was the cause of the improvement. Quasi-experimental studies and controlled trials would get closer to suggesting strong causality because of the use of an (ideally randomised) control group that doesn't experience your intervention. Therefore the latter type of test would be considered higher up the evidence hierarchy.

The evidence hierarchy shown here compares the reliability of different kinds of evidence. Greater levels of reliability, validity, generalisability and confidence earn a place higher up the pyramid. Progressively lower positions indicate increasing risk of bias and decreasing reliability, validity, generalisability and confidence. The further up the hierarchy you wish to progress, the more important it becomes to partner with a researcher who is experienced in this kind of exercise.

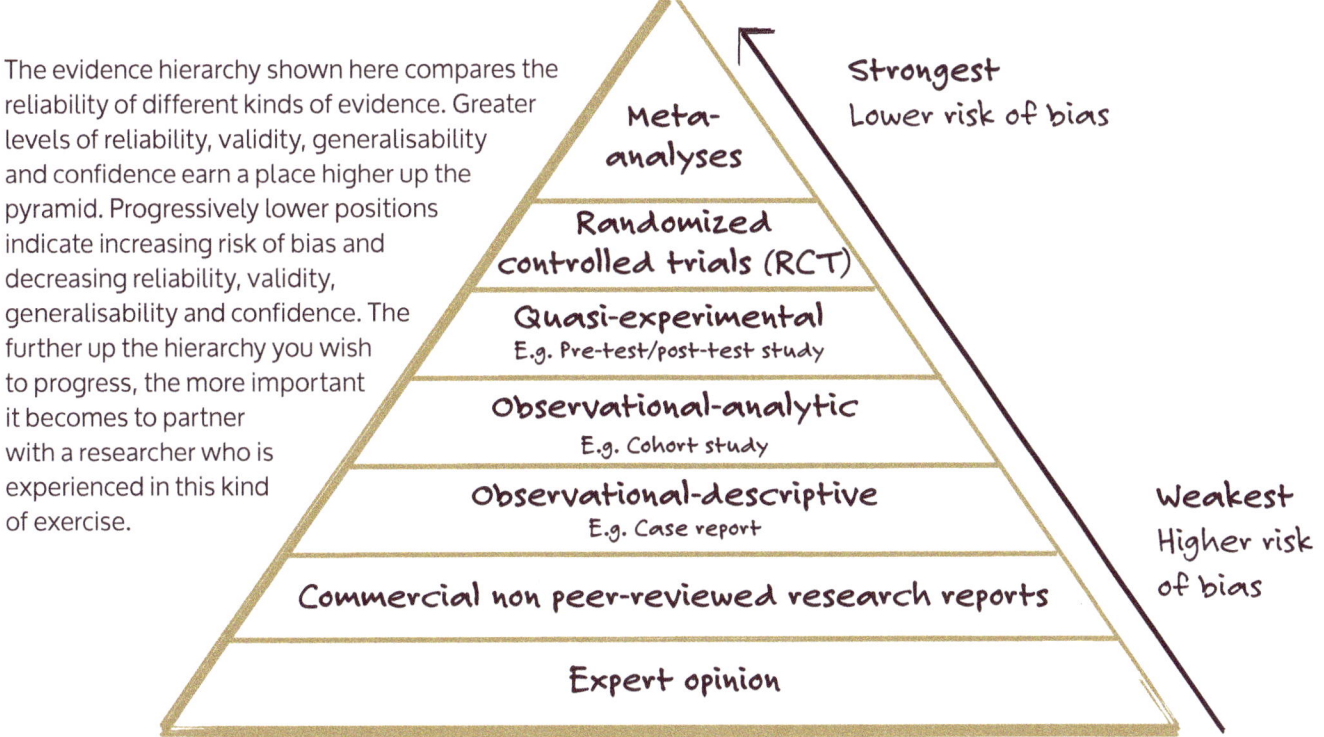

Tool box
Different levels of evidence for different stages

Stronger evidence becomes necessary as you progress towards implementing a solution. NESTA's 'Standards of Evidence' framework was developed to enable evidence gathering to progress without stifling innovation. Originally created for innovators seeking to apply for impact investment funding, it is a useful reference point for all innovators.

NESTA's levels allow innovators to differentiate what level of evidence may be sufficient for their purposes at any given stage. For example if you are working towards getting commissioned by public sector healthcare departments, you may need to achieve greater academic rigour than if you are planning to develop an app that will be marketed directly to users.

Download the full report: www.nesta.org.uk/report/nesta-standards-of-evidence/

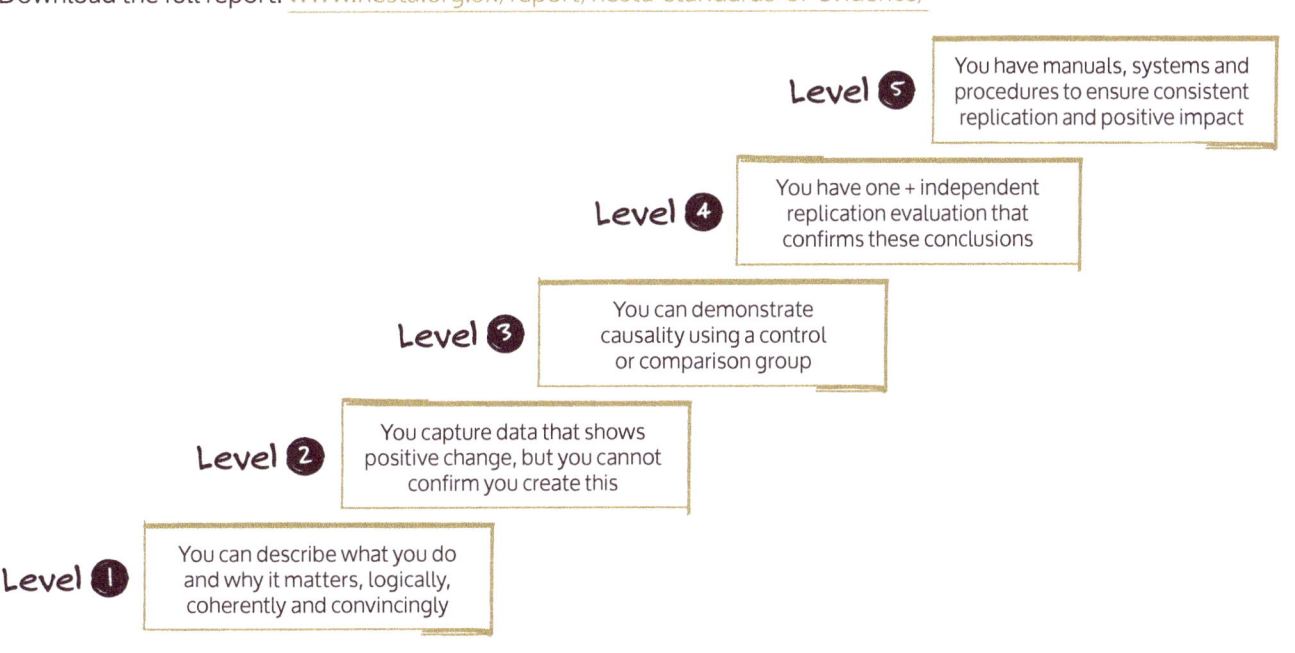

Does it work?

> **"We are very lucky to have the resources and relationships with researchers. So far we have delivered our training twice, and it has been evaluated each time. The research looked at a mix of quantitative data using closed Likert-scaled questions, and qualitative data from open questions. It has given us really useful information and recommendations to improve our offering, and the results also legitimise our work with managers in the Trust (NHS), people who want to do the training, and with other training organisations around the world."**

– Robert Marx, Innovator, developer of the Training Programme in Adapted MBIs at Sussex Mindfulness Centre

Designing experiments

The causal chains linking intervention with outcome may be long and complicated - especially for complex interventions with several interacting components. Moreover, features of the local context may influence outcomes. It is likely therefore that you will require expert support to design experiments that can provide insights beyond qualitative feedback.

Deciding what type of experiment to use demands a high level of relevant knowledge. For example, if a conventional, parallel-group randomised controlled trial is not possible, it may be worth considering the alternatives such as cluster randomisation or a stepped wedge design. Non-academics may find it challenging to understand these technical terms and the difference between the experimental designs.

Partnering with researchers

While it is more often individual academics who take an interest in mindfulness research, a few organisations have become established centres in the field over the past few decades. These include:

- Arizona State University, Arizona, US (Center for Mindfulness, Compassion and Resilience)
- University of Aberdeen, Scotland, UK
- Aberystwyth University, Wales, UK
- Bangor University, Wales, UK (Centre for Mindfulness Research and Practice)
- Brown University, Rhode Island, US
- University of Cambridge, England, UK
- Danish Center for Mindfulness, Aarhus University, Denmark
- UC Davis, California, US
- University of Exeter, England, UK
- French Institute of Health and Medical Research, France
- The George Washington University, Washington, DC, US
- Harvard University, Massachusetts, US
- King's College London, UK
- City, London University, England, UK (Centre of Excellence in Mindfulness Research)
- Max Planck Institute for Brain Research, Germany
- University of Miami, Florida, US
- University of Oxford, England, UK (Oxford Mindfulness Centre)
- University of Pittsburgh, Pennsylvania, US
- Radboud University, Nijmegen, Netherlands
- UC San Diego Health Sciences, California, US
- University of Sussex, England, UK
- University of Toronto, Ontario, Canada

- UCLA Mindful Awareness Research Centre, California, US
- University of Virginia, Virginia, US
- University of Wisconsin–Madison, Wisconsin, US

Some institutes run Masters and PhD programmes in mindfulness, and there may be potential for the early development and testing of a new approach to become a thesis project. While senior academics may not have the resource to partner directly with an independent innovation project, many Masters and PhD students use their own thesis engagement to organically bring in senior research expertise through academic supervision. In some cases it is also possible to sponsor or fund a PhD position in a particular research area that is of importance to your innovation.

Hiring researchers as consultants can be time- and cost-efficient. For example, a researcher may be able to offer you advice in just ten minutes, where it might take you ten days to get to the same level of understanding about a specific aspect of your testing.

A more extensive list of academic research centres can be found on the Mind & Life website – www.mindandlife.org/community/. Mind & Life (and Mind & Life Europe esri.mindandlife-europe.org/) specialise in integrating science with contemplative practice and wisdom traditions. They hold networks of experts and provide connection opportunities for academics and innovators, as well as distributing small grants.

Case study
Cambridge University teaching mindfulness to students: collaboration between an innovator, funder and researcher

Cambridge University counselling service wanted to introduce a class to help support the mental health of students during exam time. They ran some relaxation and mindfulness classes which proved popular, so they hired a full time teacher and expanded the offering. Although popular, they wanted to check if the classes were having the desired effect before potentially investing further. They enlisted researchers from the university pyschiatry department to test and evaluate the course.

The researchers recommended a randomised control trial as the experimental design. Among the challenges was how to conduct research while the mindfulness classes were running as normal, without changing the content or timings. The researchers used the waiting list group as a control group, compared with the group that attended the classes. The result indicated that mindfulness did reduce psychological distress during exam time.

The results were shared with the decision-making authorities including the treasurer of the university, and the course received further investment. The researchers published a paper about it. The course is now being offered to over 200 students every term. Further collaborations between the different groups involved in this process are being considered.

Research paper:
www.thelancet.com/journals/lanpub/article/PIIS2468-2667(17)30231-1/fulltext

"There were quite a few moments where we had to negotiate between the innovators and the researchers. For example the innovators wanted to know 'does this work?' so that a decision could be made about whether to fund the mindfulness programme or not, whereas the researchers were also interested in 'how does this work?' and the scientific mechanism behind it. We found that as researchers we sometimes speak in cryptic ways so we need to pause and explain ourselves. For the partnership to work well it is really important to have a clear research question and to clarify all the elements of the experiment in advance so everyone knows what to expect."

– *Julieta Galante, lead researcher in this programme at Cambridge University*

Does it work?

Securing research funding

Once you have obtained preliminary evidence that your innovation works, funders may be interested in supporting further research and development. Few private social investors are currently funding mindfulness innovation specifically, but the landscape is changing.

Below is a list of funders who are interested in the mental health space more generally. It is important to understand the objectives of any funder and how this may influence the direction of your work. For example, grant funders will be looking for evidence of particular kinds of impact in the public interest, public funders are usually also very keen on cost-effectiveness, and commercial funders will be seeking a financial return on their investment.

It can be helpful to contact the researcher you'd like to collaborate with before you write a funding application, as they may be experienced in writing successful applications.

Explore further
Potential funders

Whilst some of these funders may not respond to all unsolicited contact, they may be a great source of advice and support if your own work aligns with their mission.

Funder	Website	Areas of interest
Big Lottery Fund	www.biglotteryfund.org.uk/	Research and mental health
Charles Hayward Foundation	www.charleshaywardfoundation.org.uk/guidelines/	Social and criminal justice with focus on youth rehabilitation
CHK Charities	www.chkcharities.co.uk/	Welfare and specific research
Comic Relief	www.comicrelief.com/funding/	All research and treatment
Dunhill Medical Trust	dunhillmedical.org.uk/	Academic and clinical research
Evolve Foundation	evolvevf.com	Consciousness, internal suffering
Fetzer Institute	fetzer.org/	Human flourishing, inner work
Garfield West Foundation	garfieldweston.org/apply-to-us/grant-guidelines/	Health, Community
Hart Knowe Trust	hartknowe.org	Development of human potential
John Lyon's Charity	jlc.london/grants/grant-policies/grant-giving-principles/	Youth under 25
John Templeton Foundation	www.templeton.org/grants	Character Development
Leverhulme Trust	www.leverhulme.ac.uk/funding/grant-funding	All research
Mind & Life Institute	www.mindandlife.org/grants/peace-grants/	Prosociality, Empathy, Altruism, Compassion, and Ethics (PEACE).
NHS Foundation Trusts	NA	Research
Nuffield Foundation	www.nuffieldfoundation.org/apply-for-funding	Health Funding
The Inner Foundation	www.theinnerfoundation.org/	Inner health for emerging adults
The Pixel Fund	www.pixelfund.org.uk/	Psychological, mental and neurological diseases and disorders
The Rayne Foundation	www.raynefoundation.org.uk/grants/uk/	Youth and geriatric mental health
The Robertson Trust	www.therobertsontrust.org.uk/what-we-fund/funding-strands/care-and-wellbeing/	Care and wellbeing
Wellcome Trust	wellcome.ac.uk/funding	All research, mental health

Case study
Mindsciences.com
Securing funding that integrates research and innovation

Mindsciences.com is a start-up company founded in 2012 by Dr. Jud Brewer, who is also the Director of Research and Innovation at the Mindfulness Center and associate professor in psychiatry at the School of Medicine at Brown University.

Dr. Brewer's research lab works closely with the start-up to study their innovations and ensure that they work. To date they have developed three innovative mindfulness apps, which they refer to as digital therapeutics. These apps help people break habits such as overeating, smoking and anxiety.

Most of the funding has come from the National Institute of Health. In each case a grant application was made to study a specific area such as "how does anxiety affect sleep?". This allows funds to flow to the research lab for the clinical study, and a sub-component of this funding goes towards the company to collect the data and report it back to the research lab. The company uses the data to examine what works and what doesn't. Positive results become established in a published evidence base, boosting the company's credibility, and negatives give the company clarity on what needs to be fixed.

www.mindsciences.com

www.brown.edu/academics/public-health/research/mindfulness/home

> " The science of meditation is in its infancy. We need decades more study. People talk about artificial intelligence and machine learning, but we haven't scratched the surface of what human intelligence is really all about."

— Prof. Jon Kabat-Zinn, professor emeritus of medicine and founder of the Center for Mindfulness at the University of Massachusetts Medical School.

4.5 Additional resources

The Bond Evidence Principles and checklist
www.bond.org.uk/effectiveness/monitoring-and-evaluation

Specially designed for NGOs, this guide can assist in assessing and improving the quality of evidence in evaluation reports, research reports and case studies.

Evidence for Success: The guide to getting evidence and using it
www.evaluationsupportscotland.org.uk/media/uploads/resources/ess-evidenceforsuccess-finalprint.pdf

A practical guide for third sector organisations from Evaluation Support Scotland and the Knowledge Transition Network

Guidance from the Medical Research Council on developing and evaluating complex interventions
www.mrc.ac.uk/documents/pdf/complex-interventions-guidance/

Examines the development, evaluation and implementation of complex interventions to improve health

National Institute for Health and Care (NICE) guidelines manual
www.nice.org.uk/process/pmg6/chapter/reviewing-the-evidence

Contains a useful section on the steps involved in reviewing evidence.

Department for International Development (DFID) – How to Note: Assessing the Strength of Evidence
www.gov.uk/government/publications/how-to-note-assessing-the-strength-of-evidence

Designed for those working on international development programmes, this guide has a general application for researchers and policymakers.

The Magenta Book: Guidance for Evaluation
www.gov.uk/government/publications/the-magenta-book

This key guidance from HM Treasury is organised around a number of frequently asked questions about policy evaluation and analysis.

Quality in policy impact evaluation; understanding the effects of policy from other influences
www.gov.uk/government/uploads/system/uploads/attachment_data/file/190984/Magenta_Book_quality_in_policy_impact_evaluation__QPIE_.pdf

This supplement to the Magenta Book provides a guide to the quality of impact evaluation designs.

Using Evidence: What Works
www.alliance4usefulevidence.org/publication/using-evidence-what-works-april-2016/

A discussion paper from Jonathan Breckon and Jane Dodson of the Alliance for Useful Evidence, first published in April 2016.

Using Research Evidence: A Practice Guide
www.alliance4usefulevidence.org/publication/using-research-evidence-a-practice-guide-january-2016/

Produced by the Alliance for Useful Evidence and Nesta's Innovation Skills team, this resource considers the different types of evidence, and how to judge its quality and use it effectively.

Chapter 5

The road ahead

5.1 Growing a team

The road ahead

Diverse skills

Implementing your innovation and growing an effective platform and organisation to deliver it, will require all kinds of different skills. For example, having created a product, you may now find yourself trying to create a brand and website, connect with policy makers, or apply for investment or funding. In most scenarios the most effective and sustainable method for bringing in these capacities is to grow your team. Many innovators find this process of bringing others into the team challenging; it takes courage to let go of some control of something that you have invested so much personal time, energy and resources into.

Questions you might ask yourself include:

"What are my strengths and weaknesses?"

"Where can I let go, so that somebody else can shine?"

"What do I need to teach that person, in order to pass the baton?"

Collaborative leadership

Some organisations are more authority-based, and others more collaborative. A collaborative leadership approach can mean that people in the team give more of themselves, leading to wiser and more robust solutions.

A clearly articulated purpose and set of values are pillars of collaboration. These tell everyone what they are trying to achieve together and why – providing ongoing motivation. All policies, processes, procedures, practices, agreements and structures of the organisation should be aligned with these central principles. When everyone can see and feel this alignment, their enthusiasm and commitment can easily outweigh the initial investment in creating it.

> **"If you want to build a ship, don't drum up people to collect wood and don't assign them tasks and work, but rather teach them to long for the endless immensity of the sea."**

– *Antoine de Saint-Exupery, Novelist*

Decision-making

While many mindfulness-based organisations aspire to a collaborative culture, staff also often complain about the difficulty of remaining decisive and agile when consensus must be reached on everything. To avoid this problem, it is important to agree how to make decisions in the team. For every decision it should be clear who has ownership, and how the rest of the team wants or needs to be involved.

One experienced innovator we spoke to named three types of people that need to be involved in a decision: (1) those affected by the outcome, especially if they are the ones who will implement it, (2) those with specific, relevant, expertise and (3) those with the capacity to undo the results!

Creating a culture of feedback

Feedback is a valuable tool for collaborative working. When we try to avoid conflict by avoiding feedback, concerns remain unvoiced and problems unresolved. Creating a culture where team members are willing to be honest and straightforward with each other can build an environment of trust and connection, leading to shared success.

It is important that all team members engage in feedback regularly for the sake of learning, rather than as a mechanism for reward and punishment. While most of us have been culturally conditioned to identify fault and blame, feedback should not be concerned with blame. Instead we can look for co-responsibility.

Make sure feedback is multi-directional: if you are in a position of authority, take care to make time for feedback to be offered to you. If you have feedback to give, make time to receive feedback also.

Explore further

Reinventing organisations: A guide to creating organizations inspired by the next stage of human consciousness. By Frederic Laloux

Inside the NO: Five steps to decisions that last. By Myrna Lewis.

> **"One of the most helpful pieces of advice I've received as an innovator is 'only do what only you can do' and to really focus on bringing depth. To this end delegation is vital. I also plan to do a one-month personal solitary retreat annually from next year onwards and consider this the best way I can lead Breathworks forwards."**
>
> – *Vidyamala Burch, founder of Breathworks*

Tool box
Practical steps for offering feedback

1. **Express your purpose** for giving the feedback – for example "To contribute to the success of our shared work," "To support you in your growth as a teacher." Purposes can include supporting an individual, a relationship, or a team in working most effectively towards a shared purpose, or clarifying whether a person is a sufficient fit for job/tasks needed. Consider feedback to be an offering, something that will support and be useful to the person going forward.

2. **Check for willingness** - Are you willing to hear feedback about this specific issue with this purpose now? It's okay for the receiver to say no and find a better time or ask for what they need to be able to best receive feedback.

3. **Share your observations** of a behavior and why it matters to you - what are the observable facts vs. your interpretation, evaluation or analysis. Offer:

    - Specific observations so as to provide sufficient clarity to the person receiving feedback to be able to know what is being talked about;

    - Tying the observations to why it matters to you in terms of purpose, values, or function;

    - Specific suggestions for what can be done to improve in the specific area.

4. **Listen to the receiver:** Make space to hear from the other person and practise empathy. Ask how that landed for someone, check to see if you have a shared reality about the situation.

5. **Practice vulnerability and transparency:** the habit to hide truth is present even when we are engaging in a process to expose truth.

6. **Make an Action Plan together** to address any growth feedback; without a clear action plan feedback is less useful. An action plan is a set of practices and activities that will likely result in the desired change.

    - The giver of feedback starts by drafting/proposing outcomes they would like to see, then the receiver responds yes or no or let's change this, etc.

    - The action plan can fill the gap between what is happening and what is ideal – not necessarily about changing the behaviour completely immediately

    - Support for the receiver to process the difficult feedback can be part of the action plan.

Tip
If you feel emotionally charged, it may be a good idea to hold off on giving feedback until you are able to name your upset (including the intensity of it!) and why. This may take some time or you may want to seek support to do this. It's important to do work around any strong feelings that are arising so you don't dump on anyone and also to work with any fear of confrontation so that you are able to speak clearly and directly without back-pedalling.

Source:
Miki Kashtan's work with iBme
thefearlessheart.org

5.2 Be a learning organisation

On a day-to-day basis there are components of learning virtually everywhere – at workshops, conferences, conversations with each other and with users. Every time someone participates in your product or service is an opportunity to collect feedback and learn how to improve your offering. By maintaining humility and openness, there will be many 'aha moments' of insight.

The leadership challenge is in designing systems and processes for capturing and integrating learning in a way that is useful for the organisation.

Key Issue
What is a learning organisation?

A learning organisation is one in which learning is embraced and celebrated and knowledge is shared and valued. Members are encouraged, trained and resourced to continually learn and to adapt their organisation accordingly. The concept was coined through the work and research of Peter Senge and his colleagues in the 1990s and has gained wide currency, in both commercial and non-profit organisations.

Learn more:
The fifth discipline: The art and practice of the learning organisation. By Peter Senge
www.youtube.com/watch?v=izkXtw1tDeg

Learning Organisation:
1. System Thinking
2. Personal Mastery
3. Mental Models
4. Building shared vision
5. Team Learning

86 | The Mindfulness Initiative / Fieldbook for Mindfulness Innovators

> **"Being a learning organisation means committing to the time and effort it takes to look carefully at what you are doing, how you are doing it, and the effect you are having. You have to be comfortable with imperfection, willing to name and own up to mistakes and failure, courageous enough to keep trying new things, and humble enough to laugh at yourself along the way."**
>
> – Singhashri Gazmuri, *Head of Innovation, Breathworks*

Share learning beyond the organisation

Your learnings can have a much wider impact if you share them with others outside of the organisation. Your honesty in sharing – both successes and failures – is important in building trust with all your stakeholders.

Many organisations publish regular 'learning reviews'. Your review might include assessment of whether you achieved your desired outcomes, as well as reviewing the processes, organisational structure and partnerships put in place to help you achieve those outcomes.

5.3 Scaling impact

Scaling any innovation is a difficult journey. In addition to organisational-readiness and financial viability, there are many external factors in play, such as the policy and political environment. Growth should be achieved in a way that is holistic and sustainable - there is no point in scaling an innovation that cannot deliver its impact after it is scaled. For all these reasons scaling can take time (typically multiple years) and require long-term efforts in accordance with a well-articulated scaling vision or goal.

Thinking about scale in creative ways

When we think about scale, we usually think about growing the organisation - the number of programmes it runs for example, or capacity of the team. But these approaches to growth can be quite resource-intensive. If however we focus upon increasing impact, we may find that there are creative ways to expand impact, while staying small. For example, through influencing policy, creating partnerships, replicating via franchising or licensing, or creating standards for others. There is a diversity of pathways and approaches available – you'll need to find the right approach for you and your organisation.

Are you the right person for scale?

As the innovator, ask yourself whether you are the best person to take your offering to the next level. Just as leaders of large organisations are often not good at innovating, organisational founders are often not good at scaling. Growth requires some aspects of the innovation to be codified and fixed (for now) which may go against the innovative spirit of creating and iterating. Of course it is possible to adapt your approach, but this shift may require hard work.

Tool box
Replication Readiness Test

This is a simple 10-question test to help you assess your readiness for replication and help you to better prepare to replicate your solution. It has been developed by the International Centre for Social Franchising (ICSF) and is part of a toolkit.

Note: If you are scaling your impact through advocacy or other forms of non-replication, most of the tools in this toolkit will not be applicable to you.

toolkit.springimpact.org/logintest/#replication-readiness

The Replication spectrum

Flexibility ———————————————— Control

Dissemination
Sharing knowledge about a social innovation

Affiliation
Forming an ongoing relationship with others to replicate a social innovation

Wholly Owned
Spreading your social innovation through owning and operating new sites

---

The Mindfulness Initiative / Fieldbook for Mindfulness Innovators

Protecting important elements

One of the most significant large-scale studies on a mindfulness programme in recent years was the "MYRIAD Study" of the Mindfulness in Schools (MiS) programme. The research involved more than 28,000 young adolescents (aged 11- 14) from 100 schools. In order to conduct such extensive research, the programme had to be rapidly scaled up to cover more schools.

Until the time of this research study, MiS teachers had all opted voluntarily to train to teach mindfulness to their students. These were usually teachers who had a curiosity and passion for mental health, and, in many cases, were already practising mindfulness themselves. Teachers for the research study, however, were recruited through a mandatory process. Ultimately, this approach was found to compromise the quality of teaching and its impact on students. In the Mindfulness Initiative's reflections on the study, Professor Katherine Weare and Ruth Ormson wrote:

"The evidence suggests that we should take the development of programmes slowly, invite and train only teachers and schools who positively opt to do so, support teachers and schools new to this teaching, take steps to try to ensure that teachers are reaching the necessary standard, integrate mindfulness into wider whole school processes, and continue to invest in further evidence-based research on what works well and for whom in a school setting. All of this will take substantial time and resources."

To learn more, visit:
www.themindfulnessinitiative.org/myriad-response

The MYRIAD study offers an important lesson for all mindfulness innovators considering strategies for scale. Growing rapidly bears the high risk of having to compromise some elements of your offering, and you need to be sure that those elements are not core to the effectiveness of that offering. In this case having proactive, voluntary teachers, retrospectively, was found to be an important element of the effectiveness itself.

Connecting with wider structural changes

To grow the impact of your project, it is also helpful to examine the interconnections between your efforts and others in the wider system. For example, if you want to prevent depression in children, factors such as poverty, violence, homelessness, and food insecurity have also been strongly linked with levels of depression. So consider how you might collaborate with projects outside of the mindfulness sphere to facilitate both the inner and outer changes that are needed for the benefit of the community you aim to serve.

5.4 Deepening Practice

Supporting yourself and your offering through practice

Looking ahead across the years you may spend innovating in this field, it is critical that your own personal practice remains a fundamental part of the picture. When asked about the challenges of running a mindfulness organisation, established innovators often respond that even though a lot of their working hours are spent on conceptual mindfulness-related thinking, it can be a struggle to find the time, energy and discipline for personal mindfulness practice. Nonetheless, making space to stay connected to practice is essential both to the integrity of your offering, and your own authentic participation in this field. The deeper your own experience of practising mindfulness, the more effective you will be as a team leader and ambassador of mindfulness in the world.

> **"Organisations can only evolve to the level of consciousness that their leaders have."**
>
> – Miki Kashtan, Author of *Reweaving Our Human Fabric: working together to create a nonviolent future*

Notes